AN
ARMCHAIR
RETREAT

FR. DAVID M. KNIGHT

Other Works by Father Knight:

Living the Sacraments
Lift Up Your Eyes to the Mountain
His Way *(Christian Living)*
His Word *(Responding to Scripture)*
The Good News About Sex
Confession Can Change Your Life

Spiritual Growth Through the Gospel
(series based on the Gospel of Matthew):
Why Jesus? *(Mt 1-2)*
Blessed Are They *(Mt 3-4, Beatitudes)*
Lift Up Your Eyes to the Mountain *(Mt 5-7)*
Saving Presence *(Mt 10-16:12)*

Growth programs (books, tapes):
To Follow His Way *(6-wk. guide to* His Way*)*
Respond *(3-mo. program on* Why Jesus?*)*
Conversion *(3-mo. program on* Blessed Are They*)*
Cursillo Spiritual Formation Program *(two 6-wk.*
programs based on His Way *and* Why Jesus?*)*

On vowed religious life:
Cloud by Day, Fire by Night (vols. I, II, III)

AN
ARMCHAIR
RETREAT

FR. DAVID M. KNIGHT

Our Sunday Visitor Publishing Division
Our Sunday Visitor, Inc.
Huntington, Indiana 46750

Our Sunday Visitor Publishing Division
Our Sunday Visitor, Inc.
200 Noll Plaza
Huntington, Indiana 46750

International Standard Book Number: 0-87973-487-6
Library of Congress Catalog Card Number: 87-61186

Cover Design by Rebecca J. O'Brien

PRINTED IN THE UNITED STATES OF AMERICA

DEDICATION

To Pat Meurer
1951-1987

AN ARMCHAIR RETREAT: CONTENTS

CONTENTS (CONTINUED)

PRAYER FORMS EXPLAINED IN THIS RETREAT

How To Make This Retreat

How DO YOU make an "armchair retreat"? The logical first step would be to find an armchair. This just means any chair, place, or position in which you feel comfortable. For me this is bed. I pray in the morning lying in bed, drinking coffee. It's a nice time of day for me. I look forward to it. And that is a key to prayer.

The first thing to do when you want to start praying consistently is to *make it pleasant* for yourself. Make your prayer time a time of day you look forward to; one you feel cheated of if you miss it. This is very important. Prayer is meant to be an enjoyable time spent in company with God. If it isn't this, we won't keep it up very long.

The second thing to do is to *find something that helps you pray* — something that gets you started, keeps you focused, and provides enough stimulating input to keep you going. Find something physical, because you are a physical creature. The best help for this, of course, and one which God Himself provided, is the Bible. The Bible will comfort, nourish, and inspire you all your life. If you use it a lot, you will begin to feel a sort of affection for the book itself. Just to see it or pick it up will give you consolation — probably because of the good experiences and memories associated with it. But sometimes, or at certain periods in your life, the Bible alone may not work. You just don't seem to be able to get into it. Or you don't get anything out of it. Then you may need an icebreaker: something that introduces you, helps put you into contact with God, gets the conversation going, opens you up to each other. That is what this book is meant to be: a sort of icebreaker to comfortable conversation with God. Once you are in intimate conversation with Him, all of His words in the Scripture take on special meaning for you. They seem to come alive.

A third key to prayer is *decisions*. These don't have to be deep, radical decisions. They don't always even have to be decisions to act. One decision that might come out of a period of prayer, for example, could be just the decision to believe: a decision to believe that God really loves you after all; that God is good and is being good to you — and that He wants to treat you even better! It might be a decision to trust, just to give up worrying about something. Or it might be a decision to take some concrete action that will help you become more able to believe and trust and love.

You might make a decision like this now. Can you decide, for example, to trust that God will really communicate with you if you give time to some comfortable conversation with Him? If so, can you decide on a *time and a place* in which you would feel comfortable talking to Him? In bed in the morning before you have to get up? Or at night before you go to sleep? In your living room at a time when no one is around or comes or calls? In the kitchen where your toaster is? Or soaking in a warm bathtub in blissful privacy and ease? Pick a time you can stick to, one that can become a treasured moment in the regular rhythm of your day. Once you become used to having your quiet time with God, and having it at a certain time each day, you will miss it if it isn't there. At that point you can say you have learned to pray.

One final suggestion: *get yourself a nice-looking journal* — something you can write in. Each time you read and reflect on this book, write a couple of lines in it. Try it — you'll like it!

So now the ball is in your court. Do you want to make this "armchair retreat"? Or do you at least want to start it? If so, can you answer these concrete questions? (Write your answers in the spaces below if you like.)

GETTING DOWN TO BUSINESS:

√1. When will you begin?

√2. How much time will you give yourself for pleasant conversation with God?

√3. Will you do this every day or only on certain days of the week?

√4. Where will you begin? (Have you chosen a time and place you can count on having each day that you want to do this?)

If you have made these decisions, then all you need now is yourself, this book, and your armchair!

CHAPTER ONE

How Is This For Starters?
Why Should God Love Me?

(A pleasant chat with me ... to help you get ready for God)

Note: For purposes of praying over this chapter later, it might be a good idea — if you don't find it distracting — to read with a pencil or highlighter in hand, and to underline or highlight phrases or sentences that strike you. (It would also be a good idea to keep a journal of the best thoughts you have while you are praying over the ideas here, and of any decisions that you make or feel inclined to make.)

I ALWAYS had trouble believing God loved me. It began consciously, I think, in grade school the day they taught me that God didn't need me. God was perfectly happy without me: He had always been perfectly happy and always would be. I really didn't make His day!

In my mind this translated down to saying that God didn't care about me one way or the other. I didn't make any difference to Him. So how could anyone say that He loved me?

I slid down the slope a little farther in high school when one night I made the mistake of asking a girl on the telephone why she liked me. She had put the word out, as girls did in those days, that she was interested in me. I called to find out just what it was in me that had smitten her heart. In an hour and a half of conversation she couldn't come up with a single reason!

I hung up the phone and began, quite unconsciously, my first serious meditation on the mystery of love. "Why should she love me? Why should anyone love me? Why should God?"

13

False humility was not exactly a weight I staggered around under in those days. In fact, humility of any kind never weighed me down at all. I knew I had good qualities. It didn't surprise me that someone might admire me. But admiration is not the same as love. Admiration can even take the form of jealousy, and that doesn't come across as love at all. I could even understand that someone might like to be around me. If I was entertaining, or pleasant, or told good jokes, people might like me the way they like performers on TV. But to be liked in this way is not to be loved. I like to watch comedians too, but when the show is over, so is our relationship.

What is love? What makes a person give it to another? And what could make God give love to anyone? Coming closer to home, what would motivate God to give love to me — especially if it didn't make any difference to His happiness whether I existed or not!

AN INSIGHT INTO MOTHER LOVE

At the time of my high-school musing I found no answer to this at all. My moment of enlightenment came during a thirty-day retreat eighteen years later. I had been ordained a priest for some years by then, and I was walking around outside during the retreat, still asking myself — after thirty-four years of life — why God should love me. Suddenly I got an insight. Why does a mother love her baby?

I might as well tell you in advance that no mother I have talked to about this agrees with my answer. But then, being a mother doesn't necessarily make one a philosopher, does it?

A mother loves her baby because she sees that baby as a *capacity for response*. (If you happen to be a mother and think this is ridiculous, please give it a chance and read further.) What else has a baby got to offer? The baby, when it is born, has not yet developed any personality, acquired any virtues, or done anything impressive. It is a human being with everything ahead of it, and that is all.

But that is enough for the mother to love it to death. The

14

mother will do anything and everything she can — literally unto death — to help that child's capacity for life be actualized. Whatever will help that tiny infant to grow, respond to life, and come to the fullness of beauty, goodness, and joy, the mother will dedicate herself to doing it without a second thought. And so will the father.

What is love? What does the love of parents boil down to?

The love of parents for their baby comes down to this: a father and mother, without even thinking about it, as naturally as the sun comes up in the morning, will sacrifice all their possessions, dedicate all their time, and if necessary even give up their lives in order to help any one of their children grow to the fullness of life.

This is heroic love. It is a love we can define as the *willingness to invest everything one is in what another person can become.* And this is the love most like to God's.

This love is not self-seeking. It is not an investment in what the other can do, or will do, or might do for oneself. It is pure gift: a pure, free dedication of oneself to what another can become. It doesn't presume to say what the other should become, concretely. It is not love given to a future doctor, lawyer, or Indian chief, a love that is drawing up programs for another person's future. This love seeks only to help another grow to the fullness of life, whatever form that might take. It is the dedication of oneself to help another be great, be beautiful, and enjoy life to the fullest. It is the pure gift of oneself without any calculation of reward, unless it is the reward of seeing that the other has entered into life.

LOVING WHAT IS FOR THE SAKE OF WHAT CAN BE

This love is not just a spontaneous reaction to another's good qualities, virtues, or winning characteristics. It is not just a "turned-on" response to something good and beautiful that has already been brought to realization. (In an infant, none of the baby's possibilities has been realized yet; nothing has yet been brought to actualization beyond the bare fact of existence. And existence in an infant is just a real, an actual, possibility of becoming.) It is above all a response to the basic fact that this person is able to blossom into undefined goodness and beauty. The desire to bring this blossom into being — when that desire is freely accepted and converted into dedication — this is what we mean by love.

Is this a response to what a person is or to what a person can be? It is both, or in this case the two are one and the same. What a living person is, most basically, is a capacity to become. Just existing, just having life as a human being, means that one has a capacity to respond to the world, to others, and to God. And this capacity is in itself something beautiful and good. It is what life is. And so, when we love a person as a "capacity for response," we are loving what that person already is. But what the person is — not only a baby, but any person — is always a capacity to become more.

One of the faults of our society is that we judge what a person is by what that person has done instead of by what the person can become. A hero is someone who has a record of performing heroic acts; but every human being has the potential to be a hero. A criminal is someone who has a record of performing criminal acts; but every human being is capable of doing something criminal tomorrow. A kind person is someone who gives us a smile and a homemade cookie. An impatient person is someone who shouts a lot. But the kindest person might be unkind to me tomorrow, while the most impatient person I know might show me the patience of a saint on any given occasion. The most basic reality of any person is not what the person has already become, but what the person *might* become.

In babies we are able to see this most clearly. Babies are lovable, not because of anything they have done, any virtues they have developed, or deeds they have accomplished, but simply because of what they are — and what they are is pure capacity to become. That is why a baby mirrors to us what we are. It is why a baby speaks to us of the pure beauty and gift of human life. A baby has a capacity to respond to life in a great and beautiful way. We might even say that on the deepest level of understanding, a baby *is* this capacity. This is what its existence is: a real power, a real ability to respond to life: to respond to experiences and to things, to people and to God in ways that are great and beautiful. And therefore, if we look at a baby as a person, as this pure, open freedom to respond, any and every baby can be defined as simply a capacity for response.

This is what the baby is, and this is what the baby remains during the whole of its life, right through the moment of ultimate response, which is death. In other words, this is what we are: every human being is and remains, and cannot cease to be until death, a capacity for response. Every human person, understood and defined most deeply, is a capacity for response: a capacity to respond to life, to people, and to God in great and beautiful ways. This is what we are. This is what we cannot cease to be. And this is what is ultimately and inalienably lovable about us. In spite of what we have or have not done; in spite of how we have or have not used our powers of free response in the past; in spite of anything we have or have not already become, what is most fundamental to our being is the fact that we have, and have now, a capacity to respond to life, to others, and to God in a great and beautiful way. This means that in every one of us there is something worthy of love, something in which others can legitimately choose to invest everything they are: and that is our capacity for response.

A WRONG QUESTION

Why should God love me? Wrong question. Love is not a conditioned reflex or an automatic response to a stimulus. Love is not the effect of a cause — at least, not of a cause outside the person who gives love, as if the presence of this or that quality in someone would automatically evoke love from another. Love is a free gift. It is a free response. The only true cause of love is in the lover's free choice to give it. Love is a free act.

This is why we are on a wrong track from the beginning when we ask, "Why *should* God love me?" or "Why *should*

17

anyone love me?" The only right question — the only question to which there is an answer — is, "Why *does* God love me?" And the answer is, *"Because God chooses to invest everything He is in what I can become."*

God loves me because He chooses to. His choice is a response to the fact that I have, and I am, a capacity for response, and God chooses to do everything He can to help me actualize that capacity and grow into the fullness of life. This is what divine love is.

GOD IS LOVE GIVING ITSELF FREELY

This is not just a clarification about love; it is an insight into the mystery of God's own being. God is love. He is that overwhelming Person who, for some reason that has no reason to it except the mystery of His own being, chooses to invest everything He is in what others can become. God can be defined as being simply the One who chooses to do this. We could say that God is the One "whose nature it is" to love, but that would make God's love look like something programmed, something He is wired to do. The mystery of God is that He is absolute Freedom, programmed to nothing, free to do whatever He pleases, and it is not just a characteristic of His, but His very identity, to be the One whose enduring free choice is to invest everything He is in what you and I can become.

SUMMING UP:

At this point we have answered two questions — if pinpointing mystery can be called answering. We have answered the question *"Why should God love me?"* by recognizing that the question itself is based on a misunderstanding of what love is. Since love is a free choice, the only answer to this question is, *"Because He chooses to."* And this is true for any act of love, no matter by whom or to whom it is given.

This answer invites us to contemplate — to just be lost in

wonder at — the awesome mystery of what God is: that He is the Being whose very identity it is to choose to invest everything He is in what others can become. Why would He choose this? Because of what He is. God is love.

We have also answered the question "*What is love?*" — although here again the answer amounts to an invitation to contemplate the mystery of God. We have defined love as *the choice to invest everything one is in what another can become.* This does tell us what love is, whether we find it in human beings or in God, but it is the definition of a particular kind of love: the love that is most like God's. When we contemplate this love, whether we find it in our parents, in a spouse, or in a friend, we are in reality contemplating the mystery of God. God is love, and the more we know about love, the more we know about God.

And we have introduced another question: "*Why am I lovable? What is there in me that anyone can love?*" We will develop this more in the following reflection, but for now we can answer very simply: "I am lovable because I have — in fact, I am — a *capacity for response.* Therefore if God (or anyone) chooses to invest everything He is in what I can become, that investment is justified." That is what being lovable means.

HOW TO PRAY OVER THIS (METHOD OF MEDITATION):

How much time do you have? Do you want to pray over this chapter now or wait until your next conversation time with God? Either choice is fine. But when you are ready to pray, do this:

The "vestibule" of prayer:
1. Make a conscious act of remembering that you are in the presence of God. You are in the presence of His love, His understanding of you, His desire to give you the fullness of life and of joy.

19

2. Make some physical sign of reverence that acknowledges His presence. You might put your hand on your heart for a moment, or bow your head.

3. Say a prayer in your own words asking Him to speak to your heart during this time of prayer and to help you listen and respond.

The method of "meditation":

4. Begin to reflect and to pray over what you have read. This involves three kinds of activity:

a) Use your memory: Remember some idea you read, or some thought that came to you as you did, which struck you or moved your feelings. (This is why we suggested it might be a good idea as you read to underline phrases or sentences that strike you.) Focus in on this idea and go more deeply into it. The way to do this is to:

b) Use your intellect: Ask questions that will help make this idea relevant to your life. For example: "Does this answer a question I have had? How can I relate it to my own experience? What would be the implications for my life if I really believed this? Am I deeply convinced it is true? Do I have any questions about it? Can I answer them? Can I remember anything from Scripture that deals with this?" *(Note:* While you are asking and trying to answer these questions, you may feel that you are doing all the thinking alone. As a matter of fact, this is a moment in your prayer when Our Lord is communicating with you very actively through the Holy Spirit. He is suggesting questions, proposing answers, bringing things to your mind. If you don't see any evidence of this, don't get discouraged; sometimes He lets us struggle on our own for quite a while before He gives any light. There are reasons for this, which we need not go into here. If you persevere in your efforts to enter into conversation with Him, one day you will discover that He has been saying to you all along much more than you were aware of.)

c) Use your will: Make a decision: use your free will; exercise your power of choice. In a free, conscious, and active way, decide whether you will believe this and whether you will try to live by it. Try at this point to make at least one concrete decision that involves action. In other words, in response to what you have read, and as an expression of what you have come to see during your reflection, *do something*. Take a step, no matter how small it might be, to bring the fruits of your prayer into real life. (For example, decide to reject any thoughts that tell you you are unlovable; or treat yourself to something enjoyable to celebrate your value; or tell God consciously, deliberately, in your own words that you believe in His love for you.) In the spiritual life all forward motion comes through choices, and any choice at all in response to the message of Jesus Christ makes your prayer real.

5. *Talk to God:* Talk over with Jesus, or with the Father or the Holy Spirit (or with all three!) what you have read and reflected on, how you felt during the prayer, how you feel now. Talk easily to God, with familiarity, relating to Him as Father, or as Savior, or Teacher, or Friend. Close your prayer period with one of the basic Christian prayers which you know by heart, such as the *Our Father*.

You can spend as many days or prayer periods as you wish on any one chapter of this book. There is no rush; God is not in a hurry, and deep conversation usually takes place when people take leisure to explore ideas, to weigh their implications for their lives, and to get in touch with the way they feel about them.

When you feel that you and God have said all you have to say to each other right now about the topic of this chapter, go on to the next one.

SOME QUESTIONS THAT MIGHT HELP YOU REFLECT ON THIS CHAPTER:

(The best questions to use are the ones that have occurred to you spontaneously as you read, or which occur to you now. If you need help getting started, however, use these.)

1. Do I believe I am capable of responding to life, to others, to love, in a great and beautiful way?

2. How do I experience my life as a response to the world? To others? To God?

3. Looking back over the past several months, how have I experienced myself responding to love? To whose love? How was it shown to me? How did I feel at these times? How did others react to me then?

4. In what ways have I seen God responding with love to what I am? How has God invested His love in me? How have I responded to that?

CHAPTER TWO

Why Am I Lovable?
Why Is Anyone?

THE PURPOSE of this chapter is just to draw some fairly obvious conclusions from the last one. What we would like to do in this chapter is come to some very definite convictions about our own self-worth and that of others — convictions we can live with, hold on to, and never go back on.

The major conclusion is this: I am lovable, really worthy of love, because I have (and I am) a *capacity for response*. And for the same reason, every other human being on this earth is also lovable and worthy of my love. In other words, I can never say about myself, "I am not lovable; there is nothing in me to love." And I can never say it about any other person either.

Usually when people say, "There is nothing in me to love," they mean there is no good quality in them that would draw someone's admiration or affection, or make someone desire to be close to them. They feel that their looks are not appealing, their personalities are not attractive, or perhaps even that their moral choices have been so evil that no one would — or should — care to associate with them. Their feelings about themselves range from "I am bad; I am unworthy of love" to "There is just nothing in me that is particularly attractive."

This kind of judgment about oneself is never true, of course; there is always something about every person which is good and attractive, recognized or not. But it does no good to say this to people who feel they are unlovable, because they won't believe it; or they will feel that the unattractive in them so overbalances

23

the attractive that the end result is the same. So we cannot remain with this answer — which is superficial anyway and misses the real core of every person's value — and we must look for a goodness and lovableness in people that does not depend on the looks they were born with, the talents or charm they have developed, the choices they have made, or the characters they have formed.

This core of goodness is simply each human person's capacity for response. No matter how well someone may or may not have responded to life in the past, and no matter what kind of character one may have developed through one's responses to life so far, the flat fact remains that there is no man or woman on earth, no matter how young or how old, who does not have the capacity right now to make great and beautiful responses to life, to other people, and to God. And so there is something in every person to invest in; something real. And if anyone chooses to make that investment — to invest time, or energy, or patience, or nurturing attention in another person's capacity for response — no one can say that the investment is stupid. The capacity for response is there, and the investment of love may evoke it.

LOVE IS NOT CONDESCENSION

If we define love as the free choice to invest what one has or is in another's capacity to become, then love is always justified, and every human being on earth is lovable. This is because every person on earth has a capacity to respond in a great and beautiful way and to become a better, happier human being.

If someone, then, invests love in me; if someone seeks me out, cares for me, wants to listen to me, feel with me, share with me thoughts or resources that will help me, I need not feel that I am the object of condescension. I have within me something that is worth everything the other is investing in me; something which, if I choose to allow it, will come to life and be worth a million times more than any time or energy or care that has been invested in me. One beautiful human response evoked through love is worth inestimably more than all the time and energy through which that love expressed itself.

This, for sure, is what God believes. It is what God has shown us and continues to show us by His constant investment of self in us.

And this is what mothers and fathers show us. No matter how much a son or daughter has or has not responded in the past — no matter what a child may have become in terms of attitudes, values, behavior, personality, or character — mothers and fathers are always willing to invest anything they are or can do in helping their child come to a fuller measure of life and of love. They do this naturally, spontaneously, and without even thinking about it. They do it because they see in their child someone who is able to become, able to respond to life, able to come into greater happiness and love. And they do it because, whether they have ever consciously thought about it or not, they freely accepted and dedicated themselves at the very beginning of that child's existence to devote their whole lives to helping their son or daughter grow to the fullness of life. This is the love we take for granted in fathers and mothers, and it is the love most like to God's.

So why am I lovable? I am lovable because I have, and I am, a capacity for response. And I cannot lose this capacity so long as there is within me the possibility of making one more free act of choice; in other words, so long as I have a bit of life that remains. And this is true of every human being who lives.

GOD DOES NOT NEED OUR RESPONSE

Now we can answer the question about God's need for us. Does God need my love? If He was perfectly happy without me before I ever came to exist, then what difference does it make to His happiness whether I respond to Him or not?

Imagine a mother and father who have thirteen children — and thirteen perfect children at that. Do they feel they really need another one? Let us say that the parents feel loved and appreciated by every one of their children; they feel fulfilled, happy, and ready to spend the rest of their lives rejoicing in their grandchildren.

Then the mother gets pregnant again with number fourteen!

Personally, I have never met a mother who felt she really needed that. I have met many women who wanted to have a baby, who looked forward to it as a moment of great fulfillment. I have also met parents who, at a certain point in their marriage, felt they needed another child, even though they may already have had more than one. But I have never met a set of parents who felt that a fourteenth or fifteenth or sixteenth child was necessary to their happiness.

Suppose, however, that number fourteen is born. Suppose she is a daughter who, from the first moment she is able to act, throws her oatmeal in her mother's face and continues in that pattern for the rest of her life. Suppose she is a girl who never responds, never loves, never shows any gratitude, affection, or appreciation at all for her parents. Isn't it true that the parents' whole life will be under a cloud from that moment on?

Once a child exists with a capacity to love and respond, the parents need that response. They may have been perfectly happy before; they may have all the loving children that anyone could possibly desire; but if you were to say to them, "Why do you care about this one? You have plenty of other children who love you. You don't need this one," they would just look at you with the look one gives to someone who cannot possibly understand.

This is the way God feels about us. He made us with a capacity to know, to choose, to enjoy. He made us able to know and appreciate what He knows, to enjoy what He enjoys, to love as He loves. And all He desires is to see this capacity in us actualized. Jesus said it when he told us the goal of His own mission on earth: "I came that they might have life, and have it to the full" (John 10:10). All God wants for us is that we should come to life. And the fullness of life is found in responding to everything that is with everything we are.

If God manages to win us to this fullness of response, to bring us to the fullness of life and of love, then God will be happy. All of our previous sins and failures to respond will make no difference to Him; all He desires is to see us come to the beauty, the greatness, the joy, the happiness of a total response in love. When we shall have come to this, then God will sit back satisfied and say, "It is done! It is consummated."

It is true that some of the responses we make to life, to other people, to God, can make it more difficult for us to respond to love: to what is true and beautiful and good. A lifetime of non-response can have a deadening, discouraging effect on us. But nothing, absolutely nothing while we are still alive, can totally destroy our capacity to respond. And even if it might seem to us at times that our capacity to love is completely dead, Jesus has shown that He is able to call forth even the dead from their graves. At His voice Lazarus came out of the tomb bound hand and foot. And at His voice we also can come out of our tombs, regardless of what binds us. It is never too late.

SUMMING UP:

Can I ever say about myself, "I am not lovable. There is nothing in me to love"? The answer is no, because the core of my lovableness is simply my *capacity for response*: my ability, at any moment in my life, to make a great and beautiful response to life, to other people, to God.

For this same reason I can never say that any other human being is not lovable. Every human person has the capacity to respond to life in a great and beautiful way. Therefore in every living person there is something to love, something that is worth the investment of my love.

God did not "need" me before I existed. He was perfectly happy without me. But once I began to exist with a capacity to know Him and to respond to Him with love, God describes Himself as *needing* that response. He is like a mother or father with thirteen wonderful children who nevertheless cannot rest until number fourteen loves back.

If, then, someone invests love in me, I need not feel that I am the object of condescension. There is in me something that is worth any amount of time, energy, or caring that is invested in me. Think on this: is it not true that one beautiful human response evoked through love is worth all the time and energy and even pain through which that love expressed itself? God thinks so.

I cannot lose my capacity to respond so long as I am alive and able to make one more free choice. Therefore as long as I am on this earth I cannot lose what is ultimately lovable in me. Nor can anyone else.

No matter how long it takes, if before I die I come to a beautiful response of love toward God and other people, then God will be perfectly happy with my life. It is not my "record" that counts, but the fact that I have finally come to that response of love for which I was created. It is never too late.

HOW TO PRAY OVER THIS CHAPTER:

So what will you do with this chapter? I suggest that you pray over it, using the method we described at the end of Chapter One. Ask yourself any questions that will help you respond to the chapter. Here are a few to get you started:

√ Do I understand now that I am lovable?

√ Do I understand that I am lovable precisely because I have — and I am — a capacity for great and beautiful response?

√ Do I believe that God really wants to call forth from me a response of total love? Do I appreciate, or can I feel in some way, how much He desires this?

28

√ Do I accept being loved by God? Can I just surrender to it?

√ What can I do on my part to satisfy the desire of God for my response? How can I begin to respond more really, more deeply, more totally to Him?

When you have pondered these questions to your satisfaction, and answered them as best you can at this time, talk to God in your own words. Talk to Him about what you see and do not see; about what you feel and would like to feel; about what you want to be for Him and want Him to be for you. Talk about the experience of reading and reflecting on this chapter. Then close with the *Our Father*, saying the words very slowly, feeling and tasting their meaning.

CHAPTER THREE

I Am Creating Myself By My Choices

So far, we have only looked at the rock-bottom foundation for our value and lovableness, which is our capacity for response. This capacity is what we are as human beings: to be able to respond freely to the events and reality of this world, to other people, and to God is what it means to be a person. We cannot lose this capacity so long as we have a breath left to draw on this earth, and as long as we have the power to respond, there is something in us that is worth the investment of other people's love and of God's.

But this only tells us *what* we are; it does not tell us *who* we are.

What we are is determined by our nature. It is the form or structure given to our existence at creation. God creates what we are: He creates us as human *natures*.

But who we are is determined by ourselves. Every time we make a free choice we give some added form or shape or orientation to our existence. We create the "who" that we are: we create ourselves as human *persons*.

"Person" is a word with two meanings. First of all, it can mean *what* we are. For example, if someone asks the question, "What are you?" and we answer, "I am a person," then obviously "person" refers to what we are, to the kind of existence we have. "Person" in this sense can be defined in a dictionary as "an intelligent being; a being with free choice," and in this sense God creates us as persons. This is just another way to

31

phrase what we have been saying in this retreat so far: that to be a human person on this earth means to have, or to be, a *capacity for response.*

But "person" is also used to speak of *who* we are, and this is a reality that cannot be defined in a dictionary. It is the reality in us that is designated by our names. If someone asks, "Who are you?" and I answer by giving my name, I am talking about the person that I myself have created, the person or personality that has been shaped and formed by all my free responses to life. No dictionary definition could capture this. It is different, it is unique, in every individual person. Who I am cannot be defined; it can only be known. And the only way to know who I am is to know the history of my free responses to life, especially the response I am making right now.

If you ask me, "Who are you?" in this sense, then you are asking about the person that only my best friends know. You are asking about the free responses to life, the attitudes, the stances, the choices, which make me the special, the unique individual my friends recall whenever they speak my name. To know who I am in this sense you must be able to read my heart.

WHAT I AM IS A FACT; WHO I AM IS A CHOICE

Who I am, then, is the result of my own free choices, while *what* I am is given to me by God and even determined to a great extent by accident. What I am can be shaped by heredity or by events over which have no control: I can be male or female, blond or brunette, healthy or handicapped at birth. I can become an invalid by accident, with no free choice of my own. I can be rich or poor because of external circumstances. I can even be psychologically conditioned to a great extent by my environment and experiences. I can become by temperament nervous or calm, for example, before my free choices have much to say about it. Any characteristic in me that is not there as a result of my free choice only determines *what* I am. *Who* I am is entirely my own creation. And regardless of what I am or what I have to work with, the "who" that I create is formed by my free responses, including my response to the "what" that I find myself to be or that is determined by events outside of my control.

"What" I am, therefore, is the "me" that is given to me. "Who" I am is the ":me" I create by my choices.

SOME CHOICES AFFECT WHAT I AM

Of course my free choices can also have an effect on *what* I am. I can choose to exercise in a certain way and so determine the shape of my body. I can do things that develop certain skills in me. I can make myself a mechanic, an acrobat, or a surgeon. I can acquire through study a background of knowledge that will characterize me as a high-school or college graduate, a lawyer, or an expert on the political history of the Tartars. Certain free choices can have a lasting (not necessarily permanent) effect on my psychological makeup: I can do things, for example, that may make me a more or less constantly nervous person — like choosing to spend fifteen years as a spy in Soviet Russia. Or I can choose to smoke, use drugs, or abuse alcohol, and become an addict. By my moral choices I can even have some effect on what good or bad actions I will be interiorly more free or more tempted to perform. I can build into my temperament good or bad habits which make it easier or harder for me to respond in certain ways. Through my choices I can bring it about that I am psychologically more disposed to virtues or to viciousness.

AND WHAT I AM CAN AFFECT SOME CHOICES

Likewise, *what* I am — the body I was born with, the conditioned cultural reflexes that were programmed into me without any free choice on my part — these all provide the background for my free responses to life. The choice to take an optimistic attitude toward life, for example, is one thing if you were born with a healthy body in a wealthy family. It is quite another thing if you happen to be deaf, blind, mute, and poor — or paralyzed from the neck down. Who I am is always the result of my free choices, but what I am can make certain choices possible or impossible, or easier or harder than others.

All of my free choices become part of my "who" — part of my history of free response to the world — but they also have an effect on my "what." Because of my choices and actions, my body will be different, my emotions will react differently, my mind will have more or less knowledge; certain skills will be developed while others are not, and the background of my personality, out of which I will make free choices in the future, will be more inclined in one direction or another.

In other words, after I have used my freedom to develop myself in a certain way, then the resulting changes in me become part of *what* I am. And this "what" becomes in turn the background out of which I continue to act and create myself as a "who."

MY "WHAT" IS NEVER MY "WHO"

It is important to keep in mind, however, that what I am is always distinct from who I am. Even after I have developed myself and formed my character in one way or another by free choices, I as a person am simply not to be identified with the effect those choices have on my "what." I as a person am not to be identified with my "character," or with what people know as my "personality." The real "me" is not synonymous with my psychological or emotional conditioning, with any built-in inclinations or desires that I experience, or with the sum total of my spontaneous patterns of thought and behavior. All these things tell me something about *what* I am and what I have made myself; but *who* I am depends on only one thing: what I want and choose to be here and now.

My "who" is identified with only one thing: my present, free response to life, to other people, and to God. It is not to be identified with anything in me that is an effect of some free choice I made in the past — not unless I am persevering in that choice, so that it remains part of my present free response to life. If, for example, I gave myself over to drinking fifty years ago and spent most of those years as an alcoholic, but have chosen to stop drinking now, then as a *person* I am not an alcoholic.

"What" I am is still an alcoholic, and will be until the day I die. I will always have the inclination to drink, and if I do drink, I will always be starting down the slope to drunkenness. I may even fail a few times and get drunk again. But as long as my will is firmly determined not to drink anymore, I as a person am simply not a drinker. Drinking is no longer a part of my free response to life, and drinking is no longer a part of "who" I am. As a "who," I am a person who has chosen not to drink, even though I have a body and a psychology that continually urge me to get drunk.

WHO I AM IS ALWAYS A PRESENT CHOICE

Why is it so important to keep in mind this distinction between my "what" and my "who"? The answer is that if I do not, then I will begin to identify my person, my "who," with something fixed and determined, something it is not within my power to change, or at least not immediately. I will think that the "I" who am lovable, the "I" my name designates, is something other than the "I" I choose to be. I will think I have made my "self," my person, something I do not want to be, and that I am powerless to change that. Then I will think I have "lost" my person, my soul.

It may be that I have made my "what" something I cannot change, or cannot change except over a long period of time — it may take me months or years to reprogram some of my emotional reactions, for example — assuming that I ever succeed in doing it! But I can change "who" I am, my person, by a simple act of the will. I really am the person I choose to be. As a person, I am identified with the response I am making to life, to other people, and to God right now. If I choose to be loving, then I am a loving person right now, even if I have years of selfish habits to overcome, and years of selfish thought-patterns to gradually alter. The ideals I accept for myself, the goals I embrace for myself, these are what determine "who" I am and make me the person I choose to be.

Who I am, my person, or what my name refers to, is that

self which I have molded and created by my free choices. Who I am is not just the sum total, but rather the cumulative effect here and now of all my free responses in life. Who I am is the response I am making now; and the response I am making now gathers its significance, is easier or harder now, more heroic or less, depending on the responses I have made in the past and the "what" out of which I am working.

THE REAL MEANING OF LIFE

Obviously, the most important task, challenge, and privilege I have in life is to create my own self by my free choices. This is what life is all about: becoming the self I will be for all eternity. And when my name is finally written on my tombstone, its real meaning will be determined by all the free choices I have made during life, and the final response in which they all climaxed. Who I am, and what my name refers to, is the cumulative effect, the final result of all of my free responses to life, to other people, and to God. This is what it means to be a human person. It means to write the meaning of one's own name.

And this is what makes life — any life — exciting. I may be bored with my work, but every day my work presents me with a new opportunity for self-creation, and therefore with a new and exciting challenge. I may be retired and think I have no work left to do; but if I think that, I am wrong. The work I was called to do from the beginning, the work I was created to do, and which God always saw as my main work through and within whatever other work I did, is the work of creating myself: the work of giving shape to my soul by my every act of free response to life. This work is not finished until I draw my last breath and breathe it out again in an act of total "Yes!" to God.

Sometimes the other, the secondary works we do, important though they are, such as supporting a family, raising children, servicing cars, selling widgets, being president of a company or of the United States, can distract us from our principal work on earth. We can get so wrapped up in saving our country, or our business, that we lose ourselves. We can forget that what we become through our work is much more important than what we accomplish through it. And the most important thing we can accomplish through any work we do is to help others become the selves they are capable of being.

Sometimes we get so caught up in what we are doing that we lose sight of what we are becoming — of the "who" we are creating — as we do our work. We may need a time of retirement then, just to get back in touch with who we are and who we want to be. If — in the process of creating a home, or a work, or a better world for people to live in — we have lost sight of creating ourselves, we may need a time of detachment from our work in order to get things back into focus again. Some people make this time for themselves by withdrawing periodically to think, to pray, to get back into touch with their feelings, with their deep, interior perceptions, movements, and desires. They may withdraw for a few minutes every day, for a few hours every week, for a few days every year. They set this time aside and "consecrate" it by writing it down on their calendars. It becomes a sacred time, dedicated to making all of their time more sacred.

And when people retire from work definitively, it is not to be idle, but to work with less distraction at the job of creating themselves. They use their new leisure in order to get back into focus what they have become so far through their choices. Since no choice in this life is final until death, retirement gives people a chance to review their choices and decide whether or how they choose to alter some of them and bring their process of self-creation to completion.

FULFILLMENT IS A MATTER OF FOCUS

Does this sound selfish, all this emphasis on creating oneself? It should not if we remember two things:

First, we have to remember that the self we create and that others create by their choices is in God's eyes the most important reality on earth. This is why God created the world, so that human beings could become and grow to the fullness of knowledge and love of Him through response to it. God created the universe and everything in it just so that human beings might create themselves. The process of human self-creation is the one real action on earth whose effects will last forever.

Secondly, we have to bear in mind that the only way to come to the fullness of life ourselves is to focus on bringing the fullness of life to others. The fullness of life is found in the fullness of likeness to God. God is love. God is the one who invests everything He is in what others can become. To become like God, then, means to spend our lives investing all we have and are in helping others grow to the fullness of life. This is the only authentic way to create ourselves as persons in the pattern of God.

Dr. Viktor Frankl had an experience in Australia which made this truth very graphic to him. He was giving a lecture there, and they presented him with a boomerang. At the same time, they explained to him what the boomerang is: a hunting weapon. The boomerang is a throwing stick designed to come back to the thrower if it misses its target. That is when Dr. Frankl had his "Aha!" experience. He realized that this was a powerful image to express the meaning of life. When the boomerang comes back to the thrower, it means it has missed. When it is thrown it is not intended to come back but to hit something. The same is true of our choices: if everything we do is aimed ultimately at ourselves; if our focus in all of our actions is on "self-fulfillment," then our lives will just miss.

Jesus taught the same thing: "Whoever would save his life will lose it, but whoever loses his life for my sake will find it." Or, in another translation of the same Greek words: "He who seeks only himself brings himself to ruin, whereas he who brings himself to nought for me discovers who he is" (Matthew 16:25 and 10:39, *New American Bible*).

Self-creation is an exciting adventure if we understand it as a process of coming to the fullness of life by coming to the fullness of likeness to Jesus Christ in love. To create myself as the person I am best able to be is to lose myself in helping others become what they are best able to be. (What they are best able to be includes, of course, all that they are able to be as sharers in the life of God by grace.) That is what Jesus did. The fullness of life is found in the fullness of love. And the fullness of love is found in the fullness of likeness to Jesus Christ. It is that simple.

SUMMING UP:

Can I accept this? Can I accept to define myself as a "capacity for response," understanding that if I really do accept this I am accepting three practical conclusions which follow from it?

1. I am accepting to place my ultimate, my rock-bottom value and lovableness just in the fact that I have — and am — a capacity to make free responses to life, to people, and to God;. I will accept this and be happy with what I am.

2. I am accepting that my main work in life, the most important and only really essential thing I must do, is simply to *create myself as a person* by responding as best I can to every person, thing, and event that I encounter. In other words, what I accomplish during my life is much less important than what I become. In fact, what I accomplish has no lasting value anyway except in terms of what it helps me and other people become. I am a capacity for response, and my main work in life is simply to respond.

3. I am accepting the fact that the way to come to the fullness of life myself is to spend myself helping others come to that fullness. To do this is to create myself as a person in the pattern of God, which is to make love the root and reality of all I am.

Here are some words to reflect on, words that say the same thing as this chapter:

From the prophet Micah, chapter 6, verse 8:

> You have been told, O man, what is good,

and what the LORD requires of you:
Only to do right and to love goodness,
and to walk humbly with your God.

And from the old Baltimore catechism:

Why did God make you?

God made me to know Him, to love Him and to serve Him in
this life and to be happy with Him forever in the next.

And from the *Spiritual Exercises* of St. Ignatius of Loyola:

We were created to praise, reverence, and serve God our
Lord, and by doing this to save our souls. And everything else
on the face of the earth was created for us — just to help us
reach the end for which we were created. From this it follows
that we should use things in the measure that they help us to
attain our end, and refuse to use them in the measure that
they keep us from it.

HOW TO PRAY OVER THIS CHAPTER

Use the method of meditation described at the end of Chapter
One in order to come to a deep, personal response to the ideas
presented in this chapter. Reflect on any ideas you have underlined as you read, any thoughts that have come to you, any decisions you have felt moved to make. At some point be sure you
have responded to the questions — proposed in the "Summing
Up" section above.

Don't forget that it will be very helpful to keep a journal of
the thoughts and desires that have come to you during this retreat.

Just a few lines a day are enough. It will help you at the
end of the retreat to look through your journal and see what
themes or desires have kept coming back. It will give you a
clearer idea of what God is saying to you and of what you really
want.

CHAPTER FOUR

Everything That Is, Is An Occasion For Response

THERE IS ONE more practical conclusion which follows from the decision to define myself as a capacity for response. And on a day-to-day basis, this may be the most practical conclusion we have seen so far. It is the decision *to see everything in life* — everything, that is, outside of my present moment of free choice — *as nothing but an occasion for response.*

If my value consists, essentially, in being a capacity for response; and if this value is actualized, brought to realization, by my free responses to life, then everything I encounter in life has meaning and value for me simply because it is an occasion for response. Everything I experience, suffer, or desire in life, I should see first and foremost as being just this — an occasion for response, an occasion to create myself as a person through the response I choose to make.

The best way to make this real is to look at the result to which it leads: if I have really understood and accepted this principle, then no frustration can be possible for me.

FRUSTRATION MEANS "NO EXIT"

Frustration means "no exit," no place to go. I am frustrated when I cannot do what I want to do, achieve what I want to achieve, become what I want to become. But if all I want to do is respond to life, to other people, and to God in a great and beautiful way, then I can never be frustrated. No matter what happens to me, I can find in that just another occasion for response, another opportunity to do what I want to do (which is to respond) and to become what I want to become, which is a person who has responded to life in a great and beautiful way.

This presupposes, of course, that I have truly and deeply accepted to define myself as a capacity for response, and to identify self-fulfillment with responding. If I have not done this, then yes, I can be frustrated.

If, for example, I have in fact defined myself in my own mind as an athlete, and have identified self-fulfillment with winning a gold medal in the Olympics, then I can be frustrated. I can fall off a mountain, as Jill Kinmont did when she was training to be a ski champion, and break my back. Jill Kinmont was paralyzed from the neck down, and for a while she felt that all meaning and value had gone out of her life. Then she discovered that she was not essentially an athlete but a person. She accepted finding fulfillment, not in some particular way of acting or achieving, but in the simple fact of responding to life and to others in a great and beautiful way. She became, not only happy, but an example to the world of what human life is all about. She won her gold medal, not for skiing, but for being!

(You can read her story in the book *A Long Way Up*, or see it in the movie *The Other Side of the Mountain*.)

I can only be frustrated if I insist on doing some particular thing, or insist on doing it in some particular way. Frustration means "no exit." Suppose that I get off the subway in New York City, intending to come out at the 42nd Street exit. Let's say it is a hot and humid day, and I am carrying three heavy suitcases. I arrive at the exit and there is a locked iron gate closing it off, and a sign which says, "42nd St. exit closed for repairs. Use 43rd St. exit."

If I accept this as an occasion for response, I will fumble all my bags together again, clutch them to my chest, and stagger one hot and humid block underground to the 43rd Street exit, then another hot and humid block back again in the baking sun to get to 42nd Street where I wanted to go in the first place. And all along I will be rejoicing in the fact that I am able to respond to this challenge in a great and beautiful way! I might even dream of dropping dead of a heart attack and being canonized as a "martyr to self-actualization."

If I accept to go out by the 43rd Street exit, then I am not frustrated. I have found an exit, and I am able to get to where I wanted to go. I have to take the long way around, the hard way instead of the easy way, but I can get there. I may be suffering, but I am not frustrated.

If, on the other hand, I refuse the suffering, and insist on going out by the 42nd St. exit and no other, then I will just stand there and bang my head against the gate. Then I am frustrated.

The fact is, there is nothing that can happen to me in life which I cannot turn into something meaningful and valuable through my free response to it. If I miss the plane that was to have taken me to an interview which would have resulted in a million-dollar sale and gained me the promotion which would have enabled me to buy the house of my spouse's dreams, there is no reason to be frustrated: by responding to this event in a deep and beautiful way, I will become a better person than any sale or job or house could have made me. The same is true of my spouse.

The sale, the job, and the house are passing things; so is disappointment. But the persons we become by responding to our disappointment will last forever. Our act of response can be a moment of self-creation which will bless us for all eternity!

THE LEVEL OF GRACED RESPONSE

I don't say this flippantly. I don't pretend that it is possible, on the level of our deepest feeling, not to feel almost unendurable anguish and grief in the face of some terrible events. Let us talk, not of the loss of material things, not even of loss of health, but of betrayal by those we trust, abandonment by those we love, the death of those who are most a part of our lives. Let us talk of rape and murder and child abuse. Is it possible to see all of these things as nothing but occasions for response?

Yes, it is, but for this we must go to another level. Mere personalism isn't enough. If all we have to fall back on in these moments is the cult of our own personalities, the stoic ideal of cold unflappability, our response to tragedy will make us less human rather than more.

The level on which we need to respond — and the only level which makes our response truly positive and not just whistling in the dark — is the level of graced faith, hope, and love.

The fact is, Jesus promised that nothing could harm us. He told us not to fear anything but sin, which is our own failure to respond. (And even for that, as we will see later, there is a remedy.) Jesus did not promise to preserve us from all suffering. In the same passage of the Gospel in which He tells us to fear nothing (see Matthew 10:16-39), He warns us that His disciples will be betrayed by their own families, tortured, and killed. But none of this can harm us! If we respond to these things as Jesus Himself did, with strong faith, insistent hope, and enduring love, they will actually enrich our lives!

Anything that helps me become a more loving person is an enrichment. If, in response to all the evil that people can do to me, I can love back, then nothing can truly harm me. If, as Jesus did, I can love my enemies and pray for those who betray and persecute me (see Matthew 5:44), then all the harm I suffer will be turned into a blessing, not only for myself but for the redemption of the world.

This is not an obvious truth. It may sound acceptable enough while evil is not actually upon us, but in the face of real abuse, deprivation, and death, loving does not appear as such a desirable ideal after all; and even if it did, it seems impossible. When one experiences real evil, the natural, the compelling, in fact the only human response appears to be to hate. This is all we really want to do, and all we feel capable of doing.

This is when we must look to the example of Jesus with faith, and trust in His promises with unwavering hope. We know — in faith — that it is possible for a human being to love back in response to all these evils, because Jesus was just as hu-

44

man as we are and He did. And we know that it is possible for us also to love back, because whatever empowerment the divinity of Jesus gave to His humanity, that same divinity, dwelling within us by grace, gives to us. To love back may not *seem* possible to us, and even when we are in fact doing it, it will probably seem to us that we are not. That is why we must operate on this level by pure faith, pure hope, and the love that depends on these. We just keep saying to ourselves and to God that we want to love — even when we feel we do not — and we trust that He is empowering us to do so; even more, that He Himself is loving within us and uniting us to Himself in His own act of loving.

FEELINGS ARE NOT RESPONSE

Our feelings can deceive us here. It is not always possible, on the emotional level, to feel love. Sometimes we cannot even keep ourselves from feeling hatred. But feelings of hatred, anger, desire for revenge, rebellion against God, etc., are no more reliable as indications of where our hearts really are than spontaneous feelings of affection are a reliable proof of love. If Jesus Himself, in His agony in the garden, felt so much fear and horror at the prospect of His passion that He begged the Father to relieve Him of His mission to save the human race, then we need not take our own feelings as proof that we do not love God or one another. Jesus loved us perfectly, with a love we cannot even begin to imagine or appreciate. And yet at that moment He did not feel like dying for us. He just wanted to escape. What He really wanted, however — what He chose to want and embraced with His whole will — was His death for the sake of our life. Love is revealed, not in feelings, but in choices. And even the perfect Son of God, who was God incarnate and who loved infinitely and perfectly, was able on the level of His human feelings to want something God didn't want.

We, then, have to believe that our feelings are not a reliable indication of what we ourselves really want. We have to believe that beyond our feelings there is another level of desire, and that on this level our wills can choose unwaveringly what our feelings violently reject. Only if we remain in touch with this level of our being can we continue to believe it is possible to love back when the things that are done to us are too evil to endure.

GOING BEYOND THE HUMAN IN FAITH

In the same way we have to believe there is meaning and value in our love, and in the suffering we endure, even when our intellects can find no value in it at all. Dr. Viktor Frankl was writing as a Jewish psychiatrist when he told of a discussion he had with a group of students. "Suppose," Frankl said, "that a chimpanzee were being subjected to a series of very painful inoculations in an effort to find a cure for poliomyelitis. Would the chimpanzee be able to find any meaning or value in its suffering?"

The students answered, of course, that the chimpanzee would understand nothing. "Well, is it not possible," said Frankl, "that, on a plane of understanding higher than that which our intellects are able to attain, there is also a meaning and a value to human suffering as well?"

This is pure John of the Cross. St. John of the Cross is famous for writing about the "dark night of the spirit," a phase of spiritual purification in which we must endure by faith alone things which are humanly unintelligible, or at least humanly meaningless. In the "dark night" it is not that we go against reason; we just go beyond reason. We accept the fact that we are operating on a level where our human guidance system is just inadequate; and we surrender ourselves to living by another guidance system, which is not human but divine.

When we do this, we are experiencing what it is to live by pure faith, pure hope, pure divine love. This might sound impossible, but it is in fact the goal of our lives in grace: to so surrender to the light and love revealed to us in the words of God, in the teaching and example of Jesus, that we are willing to respond to every person and event in life as Jesus Christ Himself

46

taught we should do. As we give ourselves to living on this level, then everything in life becomes, not only an occasion for response, but an occasion for deeper surrender to Jesus Christ in pure faith, in pure trust, in pure love. Everything becomes an occasion for increasing our union with Him in grace.

A GROUND-LEVEL DECISION

If this sounds very deep and unattainable — hard to even think of, much less actually do — then let's bring it down to ground level. Every day is not filled with tragedy, and every day does not compel us to live by faith alone. On the plane of ordinary daily life, how can we accept everything we experience as an occasion for response?

The answer is, "Just by doing it." Don't feel you have to be heroic; just respond to each event in your day, little or big, in the best way you can — with as much faith, as much trust in God, as much love for God and others as you are capable of giving. Sometimes this may not be much; but that is the way you grow.

And if you fail, that too is an occasion for response! Can you respond to your failures with an unblurred faith, with continuing hope, with undiscouraged love? And if you cannot do that, can you accept even this inability as an occasion for response? Whatever is the best response you can give, you — and no other, under these concrete circumstances — give it. The more you concentrate just on responding, the better you will become at it.

A college student told me once that everything that happens in life is like a pass-fail exam: you either respond to it well or you don't. I had heard this before. But I hadn't heard the rest: "And do you know," he said, "that if you fail, God lets you take a makeup exam?"

"No," I said. "What is that?"

"The makeup exam," he said, "is how you respond to the failure."

47

SUMMING UP:

✓ The invitation of this chapter is to make a decision to see everything in life as an occasion for response.

✓ If I have truly done this, then no frustration will be possible for me.

✓ Frustration means "no exit." To accept everything as an occasion for response does not remove suffering from my life, but suffering is not frustration. If I can get to where I want to go, even though I have to get there by a longer and harder way, I am suffering but not frustrated.

✓ In order to turn every evil in life into good, I have to respond on the level of graced faith, hope, and love. The fact is, nothing that helps me become a more loving person through faith and hope in God's promises has harmed me. Anything, therefore, which gives me the occasion to rise to greater faith, hope, and love has actually enriched my life.

✓ I know it is possible to respond to everything with increased faith, hope, and love because Jesus has done it. He lives within me by grace to empower me to respond with His own divine faith and hope and love.

✓ To persevere in accepting everything as an occasion for response, I must refuse to identify my true, my real response with what I feel. Feelings are not response, and they are not always under my control. Jesus Himself had feelings contrary to the will of God and contrary to His own will, just as we do. He just didn't act on them.

✓ If I choose to accept everything in life as an occasion for response, and sometimes fail to do so, then those failures themselves are an occasion for response.

HOW TO PRAY OVER THIS CHAPTER

Use the method of meditation described at the end of Chapter One to pray over any thoughts, desires, or inclinations which you experienced as you read this chapter. Be sure that before you stop praying over this chapter you confront the ideas proposed above (under "Summing Up") and reflect on them until you can take a firm stance toward each of them with your will.

THE "PRAYER ENHANCER": A METHOD OF PRAYER TO USE WITH OTHER METHODS

There is another method of prayer that you should learn at this point. It is a method to use with other methods in order to make them more fruitful. If, for example, you have set aside an hour for prayer, use forty-five or fifty minutes to meditate, then take ten minutes to review and onsolidate what you have seen, using the method below.

Let's call this method the *Prayer Enhancer*. Sometimes it is called the "Review of Prayer." You will understand it best if you understand what it is *not*: it is not a way of evaluating your prayer in order to improve it. The focus is not on what you did right or wrong during your prayer, but rather on *what went on* between yourself and God. You are not trying to improve your technique in prayer, but to absorb and really "own" what was given to you in the prayer you just made.

Isn't it true that whenever you have a deep conversation with another person, the first thing you do when the conversation is over and you are alone again is to think back over the conversation? You "replay" it. You try to understand and absorb just what took place between yourself and the other person during that time. It is true that you may ask yourself whether you handled the conversation right, and whether your responses were all that they should have been. But you are not essentially trying to improve your communicating ability or your technique in talking to others. You are just trying to clarify and absorb what went on between yourself and the other person.

It is the same with what we call the *Prayer Enhancer*, or "Review of Prayer." This is a distinct prayer form in which we ask the Holy Spirit to enlighten us and show us what just went on between ourselves and God. Here are the steps to follow:

1. Be sure there is a real break between the prayer you have just made and the review of it. Do this by changing your physical or geographical position (for example, sit down if you have been kneeling, get up and walk around, or go into another room, get coffee, etc.).

2. Enter into prayer through the same "vestibule" of recalling the presence of God, acknowledging it by some physical gesture, and asking God's help to pray well. In this moment of petition ask the Holy Spirit to show you what went on between yourself and God during the prayer you have just made.

3. Ask yourself some questions like the following ones:

✓ What did I meditate on? What ideas, Scripture passage, etc.?

✓ What grace was I hoping for? What did I ask God to give me?

✓ What was my mood when I began? Did it change? How?

✓ Did I feel comfortable during this time of prayer? If not, why not?

✓ What did I spend the most time on? What did I dwell on?

✓ What was enjoyable? Distasteful? Moving?

✓ What struck me or stood out for me?

✓ Where was the Lord working during this time of prayer?

✓ How did I respond?

✓ Did I receive the grace I asked for? A different one?

√ Did the time go slowly? Moderately fast? Quickly?

√ Is there any area I should return to in my next prayer period?

(These questions are adapted from a page given out at Loyola House, Guelph, Ontario, during a thirty-day retreat.)

4. Talk to God in your own words, thanking Him for the lights and graces of the prayer period, promising your response, asking help for the future, etc.

Note: Don't be disturbed if you find it hard to answer some of these questions. Give the best answer you can in a short time and pass on. The goal of all the questions is just to help you see more clearly what went on between yourself and God during your prayer. It is not important to answer them all with perfect clarity. They are not a survey or an exam. Their purpose is not to help you accumulate information but to put you in touch with what God was doing for you and how you were responding to Him during your prayer period. The individual questions are just meant as a help to this. They are like different keys on a key chain: not all will work for a particular meditation, but one or two of them might open it up for you.

CHAPTER FIVE

A Look Back And Gathering Together

(Pinpointing authentic response)

How HAVE YOU been doing on this retreat?

Well, how are you to know? What are you to judge by? Do you feel you are going too slowly? Don't worry about that; there is all the time in the world. The important thing is not how fast you go, but how deeply you listen and respond.

You also might be tempted to judge yourself by how much enthusiasm you feel. Are you saying, "I'm not getting turned on. What is wrong?" and does that mean the retreat is not working?

Well, suppose the opposite is true. Suppose you are feeling very excited about what you have read and seen. Does that mean the retreat is working well? Not necessarily.

The important thing is not how your emotions respond, but how you respond. The goal of the retreat is not to get turned on, but to *turn to* something. You can turn to something different, or you can turn upwards to a higher level of what you are already moving toward. And the word for "turning to" is "conversion." If you have turned your will toward something, if you have redirected your life in any way, or raised your sights a little, then you are "converting," you are "turning to" whatever it is you are choosing.

UNDERSTANDING — APPRECIATION — EMBODIMENT

This presupposes three things: First, that you have *understood* something you did not understand before, or that you have understood it more clearly. You cannot really choose something more strongly unless you see more clearly what it is and what it can do for you.

Secondly, before you can choose anything more deeply, you have to *appreciate* it more. Mere abstract or technical understanding is not enough; you have to have a "taste" for what you have understood; you have to experience in some way its meaning and value for you personally.

Very often this appreciation is accompanied by deep feeling or emotion; when it is, that is called the grace of "consolation," and it is a valuable gift from God. It is something we should ask for, because of the help it gives us in choosing to respond to God. But consolation as such is not yet conversion; it is not yet response. It is true that we cannot respond deeply to anything unless we have deep appreciation for it. But it is possible to have deep appreciation for something without a constant feeling for it. Feeling is not the same as appreciation, and appreciation is not the same as response. Response is an act of the will. It presupposes understanding and appreciation — and a deeper response to Jesus Christ presupposes deeper understanding of who He is, and deeper appreciation of what relationship with Him can do for our lives. But understanding and appreciation are not in themselves conversions. They are not yet authentic response.

The response we are looking for in this retreat, and the only response that ultimately counts, is the response of *choices*. What we choose is what we are. Every authentic response to the good news of Jesus is an act of acceptance by the will: a choice to believe in Him, a choice to place all our hopes for fulfillment in what He promises; a choice to surrender our lives to His service in love.

But choices are not fully real until they are expressed in *action*. And therefore, the third and final thing that is presupposed for authentic conversion or response is some act of choice that is *concrete*, that is *embodied in space and time*; some decision; some response of the will that takes flesh in action.

It is important to notice that this concrete decision and external action are not themselves the conversion; they are rather the fruit of the conversion, and the sign or proof that the conversion itself is real. Until an interior conversion expresses itself in action we cannot know that it has really taken place. And until our interior word of response becomes a word made flesh in action, it has not come to full realization; it is not complete.

ACTION EXPRESSES CHOICE

I don't want to make this explanation needlessly complicated, but unless we understand the difference between choosing something — an ideal, for example — and carrying out that decision in action, we will get very confused later on.

The real conversion is an interior act of acceptance. I might deeply accept Jesus Christ, for example, as Lord and Savior, and decide to live my whole life in response to Him. Or I might reflect on something Jesus taught and embrace it sincerely in my heart as an ideal I wish to live by — the ideal of perfect honesty, for example, or perfect purity, or perfect love. And I may give expression to this choice in some very real, concrete actions. But on the plane of action I may still fall very far short of achieving the ideal in practice. I may have years of contrary habits and patterns of behavior to reverse. Or I may struggle with temptations that are particularly difficult for me to overcome. I should not conclude from my failure to live the ideal perfectly in practice that I have not sincerely embraced it from the heart. Humbling as it may be for us to admit it, we simply are not always able to do the good that we choose to do. We are not completely at one with ourselves. We are divided, and what we embrace with our wills and hearts, our appetites and other desires may oppose with desperate vigor. (See St. Paul on this: Romans, chapter seven.)

An interior choice will always express itself in action in some way. However, the expression of a conversion in action may not always take the form we might expect. Sometimes our actions may seem to deny a conversion which nevertheless is real. At other times our actions may seem to express a conversion which in fact has not yet taken place. An authentic conversion always expresses itself in action, but we are not always able to judge accurately what a particular action expresses.

That is why it is important for us to be very clear about the difference between sincere acceptance of an ideal, or sincere love of another person (Jesus Christ, for example), and the expression of this love and acceptance in action. If we do not give any external expression at all to our interior choice — if it does not affect our behavior in any way — probably the choice never happened. But we simply cannot judge ourselves (or anyone else) by external actions alone. External actions are the expressions of our interior reality, it is true; but we cannot always be sure just what reality it is within us that certain particular actions are expressing. It might be our free, personal response, whether of acceptance or rejection; or it might be a conditioned, cultural reaction. Or it might be some woundedness in ourselves that we are hardly even aware of, much less able to identify. External actions are always the expression of something real and active within us, but we cannot always perceive exactly what this is.

This works both ways: sins and failings are not necessarily a sign that our conversion is not authentic; and good behavior is not always a sign that it is. The mistake of the Pharisees was that they didn't see this. They put all their focus on external behavior, on rule observance. And so they appeared outwardly to be very religious people, but our Lord said of them that they were like whitewashed tombs, or cups washed only on the outside (see Matthew 23: 25-27). The inside is what counts.

SUMMING UP:

So how are you doing on this retreat? To answer that, ask yourself first what you have understood and appreciated more than before:

✓ Do I understand anything now more clearly than I did before? What is it?

✓ In particular, have I any clearer understanding of what love is?

✓ Do I have any clearer insight into frustration?

✓ Is there anything I appreciate or value now more than I did before?

Now ask yourself what choices you have made:

✓ What have I deeply decided to believe?

✓ To center my hopes on?

✓ Have I made any choices with regard to loving others? Myself?

✓ Have I decided to treat everything in life as an occasion for response? Have I made this decision specific in any way?

✓ In what concrete, external actions have I expressed these choices? What has changed externally in my behavior since I began this retreat?

The answers to these questions will tell you how you are doing. If you are doing well, rejoice in it and move on. If you don't think you are doing so well, go back over the thoughts of the preceding chapters until you can answer the questions in a definite and positive way. And may the grace of the Holy Spirit be with you!

HOW TO PRAY OVER THIS CHAPTER

You might first try reflecting on the questions above, using the method for meditation explained at the end of Chapter One.

However, it might also help to make a review of the whole retreat thus far, using the questions below. They are based on the seven "gifts of the Holy Spirit." They are meant as aids to help us become aware of how the Holy Spirit has acted on us during the retreat, and what we have received so far. (*Note:* These same questions can be used as an alternative form of the *Prayer Enhancer* described at the end of Chapter Four. Just substitute the words "prayer period" wherever the word "retreat" appears. Likewise, they could be used to review the fruit gained from reading each chapter of this or another book. Just substitute the word "chapter" for "retreat."

REVIEW QUESTIONS: BASED ON THE GIFTS OF THE HOLY SPIRIT

1. What have I seen or understood more clearly through this retreat? (UNDERSTANDING)

2. What have I felt or appreciated more deeply? (WISDOM)

3. What have I learned that is of practical value for me? — that is, that I can use on the level of my concrete, day-to-day decisions? (KNOWLEDGE)

4. Has this retreat cast any new light on any more complex or difficult problems that I deal with in my life? (COUNSEL)

5. Has this retreat given me new strength or courage to confront what is difficult or threatening in my life? (FORTITUDE)

6. Has this retreat helped me to feel closer to God or to other people? How? (For example: to God as Father, Jesus as

Friend, Brother, Leader, etc.; to the Holy Spirit as Comforter, Guide; to other people in the relationships I have with them?) (PIETY)

7. Has this retreat helped me to stand more in awe and wonder at the greatness of God, at the depth of the mystery of His being or of my own being-in-grace? (FEAR OF THE LORD)

CHAPTER SIX

Sins Are A Failure To Respond

IF I ACCEPT to define myself as a capacity for response, and to see life as the exciting adventure of creating myself, my true person, by my responses, how should I look upon my failures, my sins? How should I judge them and myself through them? How can I evaluate what they tell me about myself?

The fundamental principle is this: I should judge myself, not by what I do, but by what I express through what I do.

Take for example a little child, a toddler, who throws a spoonful of oatmeal in his mother's face. In itself that is not a nice thing to do. But suppose that in the baby's mind it was just an act of play, a sign of affection. Then it was a loving act, and the baby has just created himself by it as a more loving person.

He has also created a mess, of course, and has to be taught in some appreciative way that this is not the ideal way to express love. But the baby's act must be judged, not by what he actually did, but by what he was intending to do, which was to show affection. As an act of personal expression it was a loving and lovable thing to do.

This is the way we have to judge our own actions. At least, this is the way we have to judge them whenever we look at them from the standpoint of evaluating ourselves. An action may be bad in itself and yet not say that we are bad. In the same way, we might do something which in itself is very good, and yet not become any better through it. For example, we might control an impulse to blow up at someone, but only because we are afraid of a confrontation. Then what our self-control expresses is not patience or charity but cowardice. Our actions are always in some way an expression of ourselves, but what they express is not always obvious.

A SPECULATION ABOUT "GRAVE MATTER"

Let's take a more serious example. Suppose two sailors get off a ship in a foreign port and spend the night in a brothel making use of a prostitute. Both are doing exactly the same thing, and it is objectively wrong. But does this action say the same thing about both of them? And does it have the same effect on both of them as an act of self-creation?

Let's suppose that the first sailor is a young kid who joined the navy at sixteen. He has practically no education, and although he was brought up nominally a Catholic, he knows next to nothing about his religion. God has never been particularly real to him, and he has no personal experience of Jesus Christ. He has been nine months at sea, feels terribly homesick, and doesn't know one word of the language that is spoken in the port where he finds himself.

What would you expect this kid to do with his shore leave? Spend it in the public library? What he actually does is follow the rest of his mates to the bar and eventually to the brothel. Without saying that what he is doing is right, because it is wrong, we can say that as an act of self-expression it really does not say very much. Not very much that is new, at least. As an act of personal self-creation it is hardly significant. It doesn't affect very much of his stance toward life, toward other people, or toward God, because he hasn't really taken much of a stance toward any of these, especially not a deliberate, conscious stance. He hasn't really entered into maturity yet as a free, choosing person.

Let's look at the other sailor. Suppose he is a forty-year-old officer with a wife and five children. He has a college degree, is a devout Catholic, and for years has gone to daily Mass and Communion every chance he got. He has deep experience of Jesus Christ and is very conscious of the meaning his sexual expression has, not only for himself and his wife, but also in the eyes of God. Over and over again he has taken a deep, personal stance with his will toward his sexuality, his wife, and his God. He has never been unfaithful in his life.

For the past couple of years, however, he has been going through a difficult time in his marriage. Not only that, but a new selfishness has been asserting itself in his life. Again and again, although in small ways, he has put his own self-indulgence ahead of loving and caring for his wife. He still goes to daily Mass when he is home, but not as regularly as before. And when he does go, he doesn't really put his heart into it. He is riding on the inertia of a long-established routine.

Now all of this could be interpreted in different ways in terms of the actual state of his spiritual life and interior stance toward God. A good spiritual director would not jump to any conclusions. However, for the sake of argument, let us say that in fact the man is at a crisis point in his life. He is tempted to throw over his marriage, his religion, his whole previous set of values. Let's say that he has in fact been giving in to this temptation, although up to now in only small ways, and is not just experiencing what John of the Cross calls the "dark night of the spirit," in which all human meaningfulness goes out of our spiritual lives and we continue to believe, to hope, and to love on a very high level, but without feeling that we are. Let's say that this man really is inclining, on the level of his true freedom and will, to give up his marriage and his religion, his wife and his God.

In his case, going to the brothel might possibly be the action in which his deeper decision is actually made. It may be that for him going to the brothel was the action that expressed — and made real — a decision to leave his wife, give up his religion, and live by a whole new set of values.

This may or may not be a very unlikely case. I have tried to make it an extreme example. The point is that one and the same action, that of spending the night with a prostitute, expressed two radically different things in the lives of these two men. In the case of the young sailor, it was not a particularly deep, self-orienting action. It was not very significant in the light of what it expressed. But in the case of the older man, the action expressed a real turning point in his life, a real turning away from his wife and from God. In terms of what his action says about him, the second man has more to be concerned about.

Of course, for either man the action could raise some soul-searching questions. For either one this sin could be the occasion for a deeper conversion to God. The young sailor might be inspired by the experience to do some deep thinking about the absence of any moral values in his life. He might see himself for the first time as the immature, unfree, unawakened moral drifter that he is, and he might be moved to do something about it. The older sailor might wake up the next morning shocked at what he had descended to, and as a result do a full-speed reverse before going over the cliff.

The conclusion to which all of this leads us is that we cannot judge ourselves, or the significance of our moral failings or sins, by the simple fact of how good or bad the action is in itself. We have to look at what the choice of this action expresses when it is made by us, in our particular set of circumstances, given our particular state of soul.

This is both a comforting doctrine and a sobering doctrine. Suppose, for example, that we have done things in the past which caused terrible pain to others, although at the time we did not understand or appreciate how much pain they would cause. When we look back on the results of our actions, we are horrified. And we tend to judge ourselves, our own guilt, by how much pain we have caused or damage we have done. This is a mistake. What we are guilty of, and what we are as persons, is determined, not by what we have done, but by what our actions said of us, what they expressed in terms of attitudes, values, and response to the world, at the time we performed them.

WHAT IS "SUFFICIENT KNOWLEDGE"?

Suppose a high-school boy drives home from school every day doing fifty miles per hour in a residential neighborhood. He knows he is speeding. He knows it is illegal. He knows it is dangerous.

Or does he? How truly aware is he? How much does he really appreciate the truth that he could kill somebody by going that fast?

Suppose one day a four-year-old child toddles out into the street in front of his car. The boy is going too fast to stop in time, and he kills the child. What is he guilty of?

He is not guilty of anything more on that day than he was on all the other days he drove down the street too fast. He is guilty of going fifty miles an hour in a residential neighborhood. Guilty of taking a chance. Guilty of being and acting like an immature high-school boy. He is not guilty of anything else. But tragedy occurred.

The decision to exceed the speed limit was not a decision that expressed callous unconcern for human life at the time it was made. More than anything else, it expressed immaturity. The high-school boy may tend to blame himself for killing a child, and to call himself a "murderer," or to ask how he could have had so little concern for human life. But in reality all his fast driving expressed, all it said then and still says of him after this tragedy, is that he was immaturely willing to take a chance by going over the speed limit. His fast driving on that tragic day was no different as an act of response to the world, to other people, and to God than it was on any other day. And it made him no different as a person. It made him no better or worse, no more or less guilty of anything, than it did every other day.

If, however, the boy continues to drive fifty miles an hour through town on the day after the accident, this says something more significant. Before the accident the boy did not really know — not with real knowledge — how dangerous it was to speed. He knew it theoretically, but he had no real appreciation of what it meant. In the language of the old Baltimore catechism, we might say that he did not have "sufficient knowledge" of what speeding meant to be guilty of "mortal sin" by doing it. On the day after the accident, however, he is very much aware, and he has a very real knowledge, of what the choice to speed implies. If he chooses again to speed while he is conscious of all this, that decision might well be mortal sin.*

HINDSIGHT CAN BE MISLEADING

This same line of reasoning applies to mistakes we have made in the past. When I was studying philosophy, our ethics professor proposed the following example: A married couple is deciding where to go for their summer vacation. The husband wants to go to the mountains, the wife to the seashore. The husband finally gives in and they go to the seashore. There one of the children drowns. The wife begins to accuse herself and to say that it is all her fault: "I insisted we go to the shore; if I hadn't done that our child would not have drowned. I should have known better. I am responsible for his death!"

Question: was the wife guilty of a mistake — even a sincere, honest mistake — in judgment? The answer is no. At the time the decision was made to go to the shore, it was a good decision; just as good a decision as going to the mountains would have been. The fact that an accident happened later does not affect the quality of the decision at the time it was made. If the family had gone to the mountains, a child might have fallen off a cliff, and that was just as much a possibility at the time the decision was made as drowning was.

---

* For a deeper explanation of this, see John Cardinal Newman's *The Grammar of Assent*, in which Newman explains the difference between "real" knowledge and "notional" knowledge. See also C.S. Lewis, *The Screwtape Letters*, in which the master devil instructs the apprentice devil to downplay the seriousness of a sin to his "patient" while he is tempting him to commit it, and to exaggerate its seriousness after the sin is committed in order to make him despair of forgiveness or healing.

A PRINCIPLE OF JUDGMENT

The point of all these examples is that we have to stop judging our sins (or the sins of others) just by the fact of how bad an action is in itself, and we have to look instead to what the choice to perform that action expressed, what kind of self-creating response it was, at the time it was made.

One final example: Suppose a girl gets pregnant as a teenager, unmarried, and still in school. In the panic of the moment, or perhaps without "panic," but under the pressure of fear, and perhaps also under some pressure from her parents (spoken or not), she decides to have an abortion. Many years later, she has become a mature adult. She thinks about life in a much more self-determining way. She is used to identifying her own principles in her mind and acting out of them. She has become free of social pressures — so free that she has almost forgotten what it is like to act out of fear of what others will think about her. Now she looks back on the abortion that she had, and the natural trap for her to fall into is to judge that decision as if she had made it with the same self-determining freedom and maturity that she now enjoys. She judges her action — and herself — as if making that decision then were the same reality that it would be if she made the same choice now. This is a big mistake. What any choice says about a person, and what that choice creates a person to be, is what it expresses at the time it is made. And this is determined, not only by the objective seriousness of the action itself, but by the real level of understanding and of freedom out of which the decision was made at the time. It is not determined, not in any way, by the way a person is able to perceive the action or evaluate the choice *after* it is made.

This principle, if we can accept it, may help us deal with some of the tragic mistakes or faults of our past. It may help us not to be so hard on ourselves when we start thinking of all the damage we may have caused in this world or the good we may have failed to do. We should not judge our past actions in the light of what we know today, or as if they said the same thing about us then that they would say now if we chose to do them again. And we should remember that a choice made under pressure, or fear, or in the heat of passion, or when we are terribly confused, is not the same choice that appears to us when we look back on it a year later, sitting calmly and peacefully in our living rooms. In terms of what it expressed or created us to be as persons at the time it was made, it was simply not the same choice that we see now.

NOT A SOURCE OF COMPLACENCY

This principle works both ways, however. Suppose we look at our lives now, at our ordinary daily choices and our established routine of family and social life, of business and religious observances. Suppose we ask, "What is it that I myself am expressing through all of these actions and choices? What deep, personal response to life, to other people, and to God am I making within each one of these choices and actions?"

Jesus corrected the Pharisees, not because of what they were doing, but because of the attitude of heart their actions expressed or did not express. The Pharisees' religious acts were not an expression of heartfelt response to God. They were not responses of deep faith, hope, and love. And many of our religious acts may be something like them: we may not be very deeply, very consciously, or very personally aware of what we are expressing through them. This could bear looking into.

For example, how significant an act is it when you go to Mass? Does this express, every time you do it, a deep orientation of your whole being toward God? Are you really *celebrating* — that is, "singling out for grateful remembrance" — the life-giving death of Jesus Christ on the cross, with all it means for you? Is the Mass for you a deep, personal, conscious reaffirmation of your baptism and of all that your baptism committed you to? (Have you repeatedly sat down and really thought out what that commitment is? Have you thought about that as much as married couples think about their commitment to each other?) Or is your presence at Mass — at times, at least — an action which, although very significant in itself, means next to nothing as an act of your own deep, personal self-expression?

You can ask the same question about everything that tends to become routine in your life. What are you really expressing, in terms of conscious self-creation, when you choose to get out of bed in the morning? When you dress? When you go to work? When you buy something at a store? When you telephone a friend or give a smile to a stranger? What are you expressing? What are you saying about the way you choose to be? About the person you are designing and creating as yourself?

Whether we are talking about actions that create us positively as an act of response to God or actions that create us destructively as a refusal of response, the value of our actions is the same: the real significance of any human action is measured only by what it expresses in terms of the person's self-orientation toward God. If that sounds exaggerated, let us remember that the only eternally enduring result of any human act is the effect it has on what people become as persons.

Let's define "sin," then, not as "doing something bad," but as a *failure to respond.* When our response to life, to other people, and above all to God is not what is should be, that is "sin." And the worst thing about sin, in God's eyes, is that when we sin we fail to create ourselves as the kind of persons we are able to be. Self-creation is what human life is all about, because God just made this world as a place where people could be and become. All of human history, in God's eyes, is just a time given for people to create themselves by choices and help others create themselves, with God revealing His love and His splendor through it all. And that is what the drama of human life, both its successes and its failures, is all about.

SOME QUESTIONS TO HELP YOU REFLECT ON THIS CHAPTER:

The power to create our own selves through personal choices is what the gift of life is all about. When I fail to create myself lovingly by choices, I am misusing my life, which is what we call "sin." In the light of this, take some time now to reflect on any occasions when your response to life was not what it could have been.

√ What choices have I made that were not a loving response to the gift of life itself? To other people? To God? What did these choices express at the time I made them? What is my life (what are my choices) an expression of now?

√ How conscious am I of creating myself in the choices I make from day to day? Is everything I do a conscious response to God? A response of faith? Of hope in His promises? Of love? What can I do to make all of my choices, even the most routine acts, more conscious expressions of deep, personal response?

√ In particular, how can I make all of my religious practices (prayer, Mass, confession, any other acts of obligation or devotion) explicit responses of my mind and heart and will to God? How can I become more aware and more conscious of what these actions mean in themselves and of what I am expressing when I perform them?

A PRAYER FORM TO HELP YOU MAKE
ALL OF YOUR PRAYERS MORE PERSONAL:
A method for praying over prayers

After passing through the regular "vestibule" of prayer (the three preliminary acts of [1] recalling the presence of God, [2] acknowledging your relationship with Him by some physical gesture, and [3] asking Him to help you pray well), take any prayer that you use frequently and try to deepen your *understanding* of it and your *identification* with what it says:

√ Take the prayer word by word or phrase by phrase. Reflect on the meaning of each word or phrase for one or two minutes, or until you become distracted. Then move to the next word or phrase.

√ Try as you reflect to let your will accept what the prayer expresses. Let your heart go out in desire and surrender, or in praise, thanksgiving, adoration, or repentance, according to the meaning of the words.

√ You can do this with the *Our Father*, the prayers of the Mass, the words of absolution spoken in the Sacrament of Reconciliation, the words of your marriage vows, or with any other prayer that is a part of your life.

CHAPTER SEVEN

What Is So Bad About Sin?

WE HAVE JUST defined "sin," not as "doing something bad," but as a failure to respond. When our response to life, to other people, and above all to God is not what it should be, that is "sin." And the worst thing about sin, in God's eyes, is that when we sin we fail to create ourselves as the kind of persons we are able to be.

This may not be obvious. Isn't the worst thing about sin the fact that it is an offense against the infinite goodness and majesty of God? Yes, it is, but what is it about sin that offends God? It is the fact that His love for us, His desire to see us come to the fullness of life, of love, and of joy, is disappointed. God cares when we sin because of what it does to us. He cares most because He loves us. He wants to bring us to the fullness of life and of joy, and our sins keep Him from doing this.

Well, what about the effect our sins have on other people? When we really hurt another, or commit a cold, deliberate injustice against another, doesn't God care more about the damage we do to the other person than He does about the damage we do to ourselves?

NO ONE CAN DAMAGE YOU BUT YOURSELF

The answer to this, although it too may not be obvious, is that we cannot really damage another by anything we do. Nor can anyone damage us. This may be very hard to accept, especially for those of us who have been on the receiving end of others' sins (that is, all of us!), but it is still true. Nothing can damage us except our own response to life, to others, and to God. This is because nothing creates us as persons, nothing determines who we really are, except our own free choices.

As we said above in Chapter Four, anything done to me is nothing but an occasion for response. If I respond in a positive way to something that is done to me, I become a better person for it. If I do not respond in a positive way, then I have been damaged as a person, not by what was done to me, but by my own failure to respond. That is why what God regrets the most is not what people do to one another, but the way people fail to respond positively to things done against them, or to life in general, to other people, and to Himself. It is our responses that create us as the persons we will be for all eternity, our responses that bring us to the fullness of life or hold us back from it, our responses that determine whether or not we will live our lives in joy or in misery. Our responses are the only things that can really make us better or make us worse. Only our responses, our own free choices, can diminish our lives or bring us closer to the fullness of life.

WHAT GOD TAKES RESPONSIBILITY FOR

I do not say this naïvely or simplistically. I am writing this chapter from a school where I am giving a retreat to girls, many of whom have been the victims of sexual abuse. Can I say what I have said above to a girl who has been raped, abused, molested, or perhaps emotionally wounded for life by what other people have callously done to her? Can I tell her that God cares more about what her abuser did to himself than about what he did to her? Can I say such a thing without making her feel like hating God?

The answer is, "Yes, I can." God created people free. He takes responsibility for that, and He will answer to us for it. If He had not created people free, He could not have created them capable of loving. And because people are free, they will at times abuse their freedom and do terrible things to one another, perhaps to us. God takes responsibility for creating a world where this can happen.

God tells each one of us, "I do not guarantee that no one will do evil things to you, or that no one will hurt you or inflict suffering on you. I do promise you, however, that no one can really *harm* you if you choose to make the right response to what is done to you. I promise to give you the power to respond to everything that is done to you with forgiveness and with love — and in doing this, you yourself will find healing and life. Do not fear those who can harm your body or abuse it. Nothing can make you any less beautiful, any less good, any less lovable and alive as a person except your own free response to life. And I will always give you the grace to respond to everything in a way that brings you to greater life and love and joy. Trust me and live!"

WHAT IS A FULL LIFE?

I do not write these words simplistically. I spent yesterday listening to terrible stories from girls about terrible things that were done to them. I saw the hurt, the anger, the rage, the resentment, the fear, the emotional woundedness. I am not so naïve as to think that any kind of voluntary response to what has happened to them will take away these feelings — at least not for years and years, if then. It is even possible that some of these girls will never be able to enter into a happy, normal sexual life in marriage because of what their experiences have done to their emotional life. (I don't say this because I know it is true, but because I don't know enough to promise it is not true.) And still I can say to them, and I do say to them — and to you, wounded reader, wounded friend — that nothing that has been done to them or that ever will be done to them can keep them from arriving at the fullness of life — both here and hereafter.

Life does not consist in being able to have a healthy sex life. Life does not consist in having a healthy physical life. People have led full and happy lives in spite of — perhaps even because of — devastating handicaps. Helen Keller is a classic example:

75

deaf and blind and heroically courageous. Jill Kinmont is a contemporary example (see Chapter Four, above). Whether we are talking about physical woundedness or emotional woundedness, nothing can diminish a person's true life except that person's own free response to life, to other people, and to God. Life *is* responding, and the fullness of life is responding to everything that is with the fullness of divine, graced love.

I don't say this is an easy doctrine to accept, nor an obvious one. But it is true. If we really accept the definition of ourselves as a capacity for response, then what life is all about is responding. The true purpose and goal of human life, of our time on this earth, is to actualize to the fullest our capacity to respond with love and with courage to everything that is. And this includes everything that happens to us. No one can keep us from arriving at fullness of life, because no other person, by doing anything at all to us, can keep us from responding to life, and to harm itself, with the fullness of faith, of hope, and of love, even though it may take us years to arrive at such a response. A positive response may not seem to be — or may not be in fact — *humanly* possible. But with the help God has promised us, it *is* possible. That is what "grace" is all about.

IS FORGIVENESS POSSIBLE?

Yesterday I was speaking to the girls on this retreat about forgiveness. One of them said she would never forgive the man who had mistreated her, "because he ruined my life."

No one can ruin your life. Someone can ruin your plans. An accident can do that. Jill Kinmont's plans to become an Olympic skier were ruined when she fell and was paralyzed. And for a time she reacted as if her life were ruined. She lost the desire to live. Nothing else in life seemed worthwhile. But this was because she was identifying living with skiing. When she changed her mind about that, she came back to life. And she began to live life more fully than she ever had lived it before.

Living is not skiing; living is responding. Living is not just experiencing things outside of ourselves; it is responding and

76

becoming. Living is not accomplishing; it is responding — and accomplishing through that response the one essential thing in life: the creation of one's own person, the formation of one's soul.

When we have learned to feel — no, not to feel, because feelings are not under our control — but to *freely give* compassion to those who have hurt us, then we ourselves can be healed. But for this we have to be conscious that in the act of hurting us they did not, because they could not, damage us, but they inflicted the worst possible damage on themselves, distorting the shape of their own souls by sin. When we can do this we will have learned to look on sin as God does.

SINS CAN BE REVERSED

The worst thing about sin is what it does to ourselves. This is what offends and disappoints God the most, because He loves us and wants us to come to the fullness of life. This is what He wants us to understand about our own sins, so that we will reverse any direction in which our past sins have pointed us, and realize before we sin again that any sin we commit, unless we reverse it later, will have a determining effect on who we will be for all eternity. By our choices we create ourselves as persons. By our sins we create ourselves as persons who have missed the meaning of life.

Every sin is simply a failure to respond as we should to some reality: to life and its challenges; to other people in their good and bad behavior; to God and His infinite love. And because every sin is essentially a failure to respond, every sin can be reversed — and totally reversed, cancelled out, eliminated from our existence — by a new choice which is an act of positive response.

The sins of our past are like the wake of a ship, which simply ceases to exist after the ship has changed course. The persons that we are — our "who," our deepest selves — are determined solely by our present state of response. Whatever our actual response is at this moment to life, to other people, and to

God, that is who we are. And therefore we should not judge ourselves — or anyone else — in the present by anything we — or they — might have done in the past.

WE ARE WHAT WE ARE NOW

This too is a hard doctrine to accept: that the sins of the past no longer exist in the present. But the fact is that the present reality of any human being — the "who" that any one of us is — is determined solely by that person's present response to life, to other people, and to God. What we are, essentially, when we come into this world, is a *capacity for response*. When we actualize that capacity by responding, by making personal choices, we create ourselves as persons. Our responses determine who we actually are. And when we reverse our choices, we reverse what made us, and what makes us now, the persons that we are. We are what we are now; not what we were or what we have done in the past. What determines who we are is our actual response, at this moment, to life, to other people, and to God.

Of course, our present response to other people and to God includes the response we make right now to what we may have done to others in the past. If at one time we hurt another person terribly, we can hardly reverse the attitude we chose to adopt at that time without intense regret in the present. What we have done in the past does not determine what we are today. But the attitude we take toward what we have done in the past is a determining element in who we are as persons today.

SUMMING UP:

Three conclusions follow from this chapter. The first is a sobering one. The second is a comforting one — and perhaps a challenging one. The third is very definitely a challenging one.

MY CHOICES CREATE ME

The first conclusion is that every time I act, my action has a more significant effect on me than on anything or anyone I may touch by my action. If I choose to build a bridge, I have had a significant effect on society: people can now pass where before they could not pass. But more significant than this is the fact that I have become a bridge builder, and I now am whatever my decision to build the bridge expressed and created me to be as a response to life, to other people, and to God.

If I choose to talk unkindly about another person, I affect that other person's reputation. But more significantly than that, I affect my own reality. The other person doesn't really become different through my unkind words. But I do.

Choices, then, whether they are choices to do good or to do evil, follow that law of physics which says, "Every action has an equal and opposite reaction" (the jet engine is based on this principle). Every choice to act on the reality outside of me has an equal (or maybe greater) effect on the reality inside of me, which is my own being. That is the sobering conclusion from this chapter.

CANCELLED CHOICES DROP OUT OF EXISTENCE

The comforting — and also challenging — conclusion is that the sins of my past, if I have reversed by repentance the choices that created them, are no longer a part of my being. They no longer determine who I am except through the fact that they made my act of repentance possible. The sins Mary Magdalen committed, for example, no longer determine in any way who she is as a person, or how people view her, except that they made it possible for her to have the beauty she now has as a model of repentance and of loving response to Jesus Christ. Her sins no longer exist, nor do they determine her being in any way.

Nothing exists except the response those sins made possible and the beauty that is hers because she made it.

This is a comforting doctrine, but challenging. Can I really let go of the sins of my past? Can I really accept to say they no longer exist and just forget them?

When the women went to the tomb seeking the body of Je-

79

sus, they were met by an angel who told them, "Why do you search for the Living One among the dead? He is not here; He has been raised up. . . . He is going *ahead of you* to Galilee." When we go into the tomb of our past, seeking Jesus — or ourselves, or knowledge of our relationship with God — among the dead works of the past, that same angel is waiting for us. And his message is the same: "Why do you seek the living among the dead? You won't find Jesus here. You won't find yourself here either, your true self. Nor will you find peace or the closeness with God that you seek. Jesus is risen, and you are risen with Him. He has gone ahead of you. You will find Him, not in the life that lies behind you, but in the life and choices that lie ahead of you. Leave this tomb. Turn around and seek your peace where it can be found: in your present reality and response to Jesus Christ in faith, in hope, and in love."

Are you able to stop looking, mesmerized, into the darkness of the past? Are you willing to make the choice to turn around and live? Why do you seek the living among the dead? He is not here. He has gone *ahead of you* and is waiting for you in the next response you make: to your own reality, to life, to other people, and to God."

CAN I ACCEPT PRESENT PEOPLE?

The last conclusion may be more challenging, or less, depending on your experience: Can you accept the fact that other people are no longer characterized by the sins of their past, but only by their present response to God, to life, and to you? In other words, can you forgive?

The people who hurt you in the past chose, at the time they did it, to be the kind of people who hurt. That created them as the persons they became at that time through that choice. And you responded to them then according to what they were choosing to be. But are they still choosing to be what they chose to be then? Have they reversed their attitudes, their choices? Have they made responses to life since, and to other people, and to God — and perhaps, whether you know it or not, to you —

which have created them as totally different persons? Is their true reality determined now more by their repentance than by their sins? And are you willing to accept them as the persons they are now instead of as the persons they used to be?

That is what Christian forgiveness means: to accept the risen, living persons of those who have hurt us instead of consigning them forever to the tomb. Christians do not live in the past, but in the present and the future, because Jesus came out of the tomb. If the voice of Jesus has reached those who have hurt us, buried in the death of their sins, and has summoned them as once it summoned Lazarus: "Lazarus, I say to you, come forth!" then who are we to push them back into the grave? Memory recalls a reality that was. But memory is not always a reliable perception of the reality that is. There are times when to remember is to distort, even to falsify completely the truth as it exists today. And therefore we have to make a choice, not to forgive and forget what was, but to forgive and remember that what was at one time may not exist at all today. We have to accept every human being — ourselves and others included — for what that person is today, remembering that God is able to make a "new creation" of us all.

QUESTIONS TO HELP YOU REFLECT ON THIS CHAPTER:

√ Can I accept the statement that the worst thing about sin, in God's eyes, is what the sinner becomes through it?

√ Can I accept the statement that nothing anyone else does to me can really harm me, but only my own response to it? Are there any bad responses I have made in the past because of what others did to me? Can I simply reverse those responses now?

√ Can I accept the fact that repentance, or a change of response, changes the reality of the person who sinned, just as the sin did? Can I accept the fact that the sins of my past are no longer a part of my being? That they no longer diminish in any way the value of who I am as a person?

√ Can I forgive others who have hurt me, and accept them now, not as the persons they were when they sinned against me, but as the persons they are: the persons they have become through the responses they are making right now?

Reflect on these questions, using the method of meditation explained at the end of Chapter One. Save some prayer time at the end to review and absorb your prayer, using the *Prayer Enhancer* described at the end of Chapter Four or the *Review Questions* based on the gifts of the Holy Spirit which are given at the end of Chapter Five.

CHAPTER EIGHT

A Concrete, Working Ideal

IF I PUT the past behind me and look forward to creating myself in the present and future by choices, what can I adopt as a working ideal to aim at?

Very simply, I can choose to respond to every person and event in my life with love.

This sounds abstract to begin with, but let's bring it down to the concrete. Suppose that every morning of every day, when I get out of bed, I dedicate myself to showing love to every person I meet. Suppose I say, "Every person I meet today, I am going to say something or do something to make that person happier." What would be the result of this?

FOCUS ON GIVING

First, it will make me during this whole day other-centered instead of self-centered. Instead of going about with my mind unconsciously attuned to what is or is not pleasing to me, I will go about consciously thinking of how I can make life more pleasing to others. If I go down to breakfast, for example, I won't be thinking, "Will there be dirty dishes in the sink? Will the coffee be hot or cold? Will the telephone ring before I can drink mine?" Instead, I will be thinking of how others might feel this morning, and how I can help them feel better. I will be set to smile and to say something nice to the first person I meet.

As I go about my work, my mind will not be set to pick up what is wrong with this day, to criticize, to groan with that sinking feeling, "I knew it was going to be like this!" every time someone or something doesn't measure up to my expectations. Instead, my mind will be geared to the positive, to the productive, to the life-giving response I can make to whatever reality is there. I will not greet other people like a teacher giving a test she is sure everyone is going to fail, but rather like a teacher looking forward to enriching others' lives with a new idea, an exciting ideal, an exhilarating experience of beauty. When others approach me, I will not receive them with a pass-fail test in the back of my mind, anticipating disappointment. (If I do this, then my day will probably be characterized by disappointment.) Instead I will receive each person as an opportunity, a challenge given to me. Every encounter will be an opportunity to show love, a challenge to respond in a life-giving, loving way to this particular person.

LOVING VS. MANAGING

To take the other-centered rather than the self-centered stance can change my whole experience of life. If I take the self-centered approach, then necessarily every encounter with others is going to be a pass-fail situation, with the outcome out of my control. Subconsciously I will be asking, in every interaction with others, "Is this person's performance going to measure up to my standards? Am I going to get from this person the response that I desire?" And since the answer to that question really doesn't depend on me, but on what the other person does, my own experience of satisfaction or frustration will be completely out of my hands. It will depend entirely on what the other person chooses to do. This is a pretty risky way to go through life!

As a result, I may become — again, perhaps quite unconsciously — a very controlling or manipulative person. If my satisfaction is going to depend on what other people do, it will be very important to me to exercise control over what they do. I will not relate very easily to anyone whose behavior is not completely under my management — at least insofar as the other person's behavior affects me. Carried to an extreme, this could turn every day of my life into a full-time working day! I could spend the rest of my life being constantly on duty, constantly managing, constantly setting right what everybody around me is doing, like the plagued manager of a failing department store.

That is no way to live!

If, on the other hand, I take the other-centered approach to life, then the outcome of every encounter with other people depends entirely on me. If my goal in every interaction is to respond to others with love, the fulfillment of my desire depends on what I myself do. If my first desire in every interaction with others is to do everything I can to help (not make) others be happy, to think better of themselves, or to feel loved and encouraged to become better, and to know God's love for them and rejoice in it, then I can find peace in everything I do: the peace of knowing that I have given myself in love.

A CHOICE OF GOALS

This could appear to be just a subtle form of self-centeredness. As I write these paragraphs, they sound to me a little bit like a motivational tape for salesmen, or the kind of literature the pop psychologists are writing. They sound like a pep talk for self-fulfillment, like a "how to be happy" formula. Seen from this point of view, it looks as if I am suggesting we just use everything and everyone as opportunities for our own self-fulfillment. This could be a most radical form of egoism.

Actually, we are touching here on an age-old problem: Can there be such a thing as selfless love, since loving by its very nature makes us happy? To love is to enhance one's own being. To arrive at the perfection of love is to arrive at perfect self-fulfillment. To love is to be like God; therefore nothing is more self-gratifying in an ultimate sense than to love.

The best answer to this problem is just to devote oneself to loving. Then the answer will be clear. But that is the key: to devote oneself, not to self-fulfillment as a goal, but to loving. If I start each day with the idea, "Today I am going to become a better person, a happier person, by loving everyone I meet," I just may miss the mark. I may in fact spend the day in dedication to myself, nurturing my own egoism. But if I start each day with the desire simply to make other people happy, to love them and focus on fulfilling their needs, then, yes, I will become a better person and a happier person myself, but I will be living in love, not in egoism.

If my focus is on loving others in a life-giving way, I do not say that there will be no sorrow or pain in my life. To love others truly is to open oneself to all the pain that is in them. To love everyone with the love of Christ is to open oneself to the pain of the whole world. But pain and frustration are not the same. The pain of trying to love others into life and seeing them refuse it is not a frustrating pain. It is just a suffering pain. This is a pain compatible with peace. It is the pain of the heart of Christ, which is a pain compatible with the beatitude of God.

The decision we are proposing in this chapter — a decision to think and pray over — is a very simple choice. It is the decision to try — every day, with every person I meet — to do something positively life-giving, positively loving. It may be nothing more than a smile, or a thoughtful gesture, like opening a door. It may be a kind word, or a deliberate looking for something to praise in the other. It may be saying something for the millionth time that is already perfectly obvious, such as, "You know, I really like you!" Or, "You look great today — you look great every day."

A CONCRETE EXAMPLE

I've seen this principle put to work in a family. The husband and father was a man who, growing up, had an uncle who used to come to his house sometimes, and when he did he always said something to his nephew that built him up. He noticed things the boy was able to do, things he did well. He praised the boy to his face and in front of others. He always had something to say to him that told the boy he cared about him, that he liked him.

My friend (the nephew) was struck by this. At some point while this was going on he realized how good it was: how much it meant to him, how much it was helping him. And he resolved to do the same thing for others.

It became a characteristic of his personality, an element always present in the way he dealt with others. His wife picked it up from him (at least, that is where she told me she got it). And their children picked it up from their parents. The result is that anyone visiting their home, as I have many times, is overwhelmed by the spirit of wholesomeness, calm, kindness, and mutual thoughtfulness which characterizes their family life. Their children have an extraordinary confidence and poise; and at every age level (they range from college graduates to grade school) a sensitivity toward others that is more mature than their years. And it all comes, according to the parents, principally from this one thing: that they constantly and sincerely "build up their children in love."

One of their children — the second to last — was an unaffectionate baby. At two months his character was just cold and unresponsive. The parents decided that they would deliberately try to change this characteristic through love. They made a point of picking the baby up and hugging him every time they came anywhere near him. They did this all day long. In the evening the father would lie on the bed with the baby on his chest, kissing him and telling him how much he loved him. By the time the child was six months old he had become a responsive, affectionate baby. And now, as I write this ten years later, he is a self-confident, well-balanced, extremely considerate, friendly young boy.

A CHOICE FOR ALL SEASONS

What I have written here is not really, and is not meant to be, just a suggestion for raising children! The effects of constant love — and constantly expressing love and affirmation — may be more dramatically observable in children, but what we are talking about is a way of acting to adopt toward all people, at every age of their life and of one's own. We are speaking of a decision through which we ourselves become more loving, more life-giving, more like God. This is a decision to be made at any age, and one for which sometimes older people are more prepared.

I once served in a parish with a supposedly retired priest who had held many important positions in his life: college president, pastor, religious superior. Now he was in residence in the parish, helping out in various ways, and he said to me one day: "You know, I've done a lot of different kinds of ministry in my life, but now that I'm old I see my real work as just being kind to people." He laughed and added, "I sometimes wish I had begun that years ago."

The decision we are proposing here is a very simple thing to do and, really, a very easy thing to do — although to keep it up day after day can turn into heroic love. Just to resolve every day to give to every person you meet — to give some notice, some attention, a kind word, a smile, a compliment, an expression of affection, a thoughtful gesture — this is not something so self-sacrificing or costly that your stomach turns over in fear at the prospect of it. It is something easy in itself; something that takes up practically no time or energy on any given occasion. And yet it is something which can transform your whole personality, alter your relationship with everyone with whom you deal, and change the tone of your whole environment. It can even lift up to a higher, happier level your experience of life itself, That is a fact. Try it and see!

QUESTIONS TO HELP YOU REFLECT ON THIS CHAPTER:

✓ What was the constant attitude of mind Jesus held toward people? How did He express it from day to day? What is my habitual attitude? How do I show it?

✓ What do I suppose people felt when they were around Jesus? Is this what they feel when they are around me? What can I do to have something of the same effect on everyone I deal with that He did?

√ How can I begin to make my constant attitude toward others and expression of myself to them one of life-giving affirmation and love? Is there anyone in particular for whom I should do this? When, where, how could I begin?

√ Is this the attitude I really choose now to take toward others and toward everything in my life? Why?

A NEW PRAYER FORM TO LEARN: THE "AWARENESS EXERCISE"

To help us live in constant response to God, let's learn a new method of prayer. It is called the *Awareness Exercise*.

The first three steps (the "vestibule" of prayer) are the same as we learned at the end of Chapter One. The steps that follow are a way to become more aware of how you are creating yourself by your choices, of how God is working with you in this process.

The "vestibule"

1. Settle into a comfortable position and take a minute to recall consciously that you are in the presence of God. Just be aware that He is within you and around you. Immerse yourself peacefully in His presence as in a mist of brightness.

2. Make some physical gesture of recognition, acknowledging His presence and who He is for you. You might put your hand on your heart, or bow your head, or join your hands before your face in a posture of prayer.

3. Ask Him to help you pray; in this case, to see clearly what responses He has invited you to make this day and how you have made them. Ask Him to make you aware of the loving

interateraction that has been going on between Him and you during the past twenty-four hours.

The Awareness Exercise

4. Now use your memory to look back on the past day, singling out for attention anything for which you can be grateful to God. What did God give you to work with this day? Your life, your talents, special insights or experiences? Did He reveal His love to you in any way today? Through anything He made? Through other people? Through any personal experiences? Be grateful and thank Him.

5. Now ask God to let you remember and identify any special invitations He gave you during the past day. Use your memory again to go through the day, looking for occasions when you could have responded to others or to Him with some specific act of faith, of hope, of love. A good way to identify these invitations is to look at the moments during the day when your *mood* or your *feelings* changed. Can you remember moments when you passed from joy to sadness or from sadness to joy? From enthusiasm to the blahs? From discouragement to encouragement? From better feelings about yourself to worse, or from worse to better? Look at the thought, the choice, or the event that immediately preceded this change of mood: do you think God was saying anything to you at that point?

6. Look at the specific choices you have made during the past day. How have they shaped the "you," the person you are becoming? Are you happy with them? Are there any that you think God is particularly happy with? Looking back with hindsight, can you see how God was influencing you in any of them?

7. In particular, look at the effect of these choices on yourself and on others. Were the feelings that they produced in you life-giving? Were they the kind of feelings that God causes in you, feelings that help you respond to Him with more love, more trust, more courage? Or was the effect of some particular choice (or some particular thought you entertained) to make you feel less encouraged, less faith in God and His love, less enthusi-

asm to serve Him? Judging from the effect a choice or thought produced in you, decide whether you think it was from God or not, and embrace it or reject it accordingly.

8. Thank God for the good choices He has inspired in you. If there were any choices you discern as not having been according to God's desire for you, tell Him you are sorry.

9. Use your will to make any decisions that seem to be called for: for example, about directions or convictions to confirm; tendencies or thoughts to reject; initiatives you do or do not want to follow up on.

10. Finally, talk to Our Lord, or to the Father, or the Holy Spirit, giving thanks for this time of prayer, and expressing whatever is in your heart.

Use this method to reflect on the day you have just lived, and use it every day after that if you choose.

(*Note:* This method is taught by St. Ignatius of Loyola as the "Examen of Conscience." I prefer the title given to it by the Jesuits at Loyola House in Guelph, Ontario, and have tried to base this explanation of the method on theirs.)

CHAPTER NINE

A Vision Made Flesh

IDEALS ARE abstract. What we need is a live person, a warm human being to relate to, to give our lives to, to interact with and respond to in love.

We can live for a while — perhaps — on the ideal of just giving love to everybody. And if we see that our love is appreciated, the visible joy of others and their warm, human response to us will help to keep us going. But if we are living out this ideal all day, trying to give life and love to everyone we meet, the balance of giving will probably be in our favor. Or at least it will seem to be. We may well feel at times that we are giving more than we get, and that our ability to give and keep giving in love is being slowly drained.

That is when we need someone loving us. Someone real and warm and human. And someone who loves us not just a little bit, or as one member of a whole circle of friends. We need someone who loves us and wants to be loved by us with totality; with a completeness that makes our relationship with each other unique. We want a relationship with someone which, yes, we can share with others; into which we can draw others, and which they can understand and delight in with us, but in such a way that what exists between the two of us remains particular and special to us two. We want to have with one other person a relationship in which no one else can share on equal terms.

Married love, spousal love, should be a relationship like this. So can other deep, lasting, and intimate friendships be.

And it is the belief of Christians — one not proclaimed or reflected upon enough — that every believer and friend of Jesus Christ can have a relationship of love like this with Him.

CHRIST'S LOVE FOR US

Let's pass over for a moment the obvious difficulty, apparent at least, that Jesus Christ does not seem to have on earth today a real, warm, and human presence; not the kind of physical presence we feel we require. He does, of course, in the warm, human, physical people who are His body on earth today. In the Church — in all the members of the Church — Jesus lives and acts humanly today. He acts in each one differently, of course, respecting and identifying Himself with the particular personality and characteristics of each person in and through whom He is expressing Himself. In a child, Jesus does not speak as an adult; and in a twentieth-century American He does not speak as a first-century Mediterranean Jew. We find Christ loving us today and expressing that love in as many different ways as there are people in whom we encounter Him.

Jesus also acts in a special way in each person according to each one's responsibilities and role in the Church. In people who care for the sick, Jesus heals and comforts. In teachers, He teaches. In those who administer the sacraments, Jesus does what He has pledged Himself to do in each sacrament. (The word "sacrament" means "oath" or "promise" or "pledge." In each one Jesus acts in a way we can count on, and we can be assured of encountering Him when we receive the sacraments.) In the hierarchy, Jesus teaches and governs the Church with His own authority. In all of these people who are His body and His instruments or ministers on earth, Jesus acts. He acts more or less well, more or less badly, according to how completely each person is surrendered to Him, but whenever Jesus Christ acts in someone who is a member of His body and grace, we are encountering the love of Jesus Christ in the flesh.

This is all true. But we can also experience Christ's love as coming from Him directly, not only embodied in another human being's expression of love for us. Jesus is alive and loving in Himself, and we are aware of being loved by Him. We know Him and we know His love.

Two years ago I was helping to give a retreat to some high-school seniors. We asked the students if they would answer two questions: "What was Jesus for you when you were little?" and "What is He for you now?"

The answer to the first question was predictable: most of the students who spoke said that when they were little Jesus was mostly an authority figure. He made the rules and you had to obey them. But I was surprised at the degree of unanimity on the second answer: almost everyone said that now Jesus was "someone I can trust; someone who accepts me as I am; someone I can talk to about anything and tell anything to." Some said He was the only person they felt they could talk to about absolutely everything.

Clearly these students felt they had the kind of relationship with Jesus Christ we are talking about. They may not have reflected upon it as much as they should have, and it might not have been as strong as it could have been, but essentially it was there. They knew that they had a relationship with Him unlike their relationships with any other person; something unique and personal and particular between themselves and Him.

ULTIMATE LONELINESS: THE ONLY ANSWER

When I studied theology in France my best friends were a German couple who lived across the street from our seminary. Hans worked for the seminary, went back across the street at midmorning for his coffee break, took the European two-hour lunch period at home, had coffee in the afternoon again with his wife, was always home for supper, and practically never went out again after that. In other words, he was at home more than any other man I knew. They had five children at the time and were living in a tiny apartment. One day, while the three of us were sitting there having coffee, I asked his wife, "What is the hardest thing about marriage?"

95

She answered, "Loneliness."

My mouth dropped open. They were a very close couple, deeply in love, with the strong kind of love that comes from having endured a lot of difficult times together. (Today they are nearing seventy and even deeper in love than before.) I said, "That's impossible! You are always together; Hans is always at home; you have a million kids around all the time; there is no way you can be lonely!"

I looked over at Hans for confirmation. Instead he just nodded his head and said, "She's right. Ultimately, everyone is fundamentally alone."

I wasn't sure I understood this then, and I'm not certain I understand it now. But I think I do. I believe they were talking about a level of our being — the deepest core of our selfhood, of our thoughts, our feelings, our desires — which, try as we may, we cannot completely communicate to any other person. We long to be known as we know ourselves, and to know another with that immediacy of knowledge which is each individual's own personal experience of existing. We long to be with someone to whom we do not have to explain ourselves, who knows what we feel and what we think as immediately and as intimately as we do, and who cares about us even more than we care about ourselves. And sometimes the deepest relationship of love, the most open and intimate sharing with another, only serves to make us conscious that within each one of us there is a core of self-awareness where, in the last analysis, all of us remain irremediably alone with ourselves.

It is on this level that we find our experience of love with Jesus Christ.

AN EXPERIENCE OF CLOSENESS

We know — and I think each one of us knows with a certitude of knowledge that is more than just something we learned, a certitude that is a deep, interior awareness — that Jesus Christ knows us and understands us more deeply than we know and understand ourselves. We know that He cares about us more than any other person does or could — and we know this even though at times we do not *feel* particularly loved or lovable.

We know that we do not have to communicate to Him our thoughts or feelings or desires (even though it is good to do so: to talk to Him about these things in prayer, the way we talk to other friends about things in us they already know), because all that we are is as immediately present to Him as it is to us.

And He cares about us; He loves us. Even though we are not always able to capture this awareness on the feeling level, to rejoice in the emotional reassurance that we are loved and cherished and appreciated by God, we still know it is true. We know that Jesus is our Friend and our Savior; that He has chosen to be; that He is and always will be faithful to us in love, that He can never abandon us or reject us.

If we know all this, why isn't the friendship of Jesus more of a comfort to us? Why do we so often feel alone or lonely or un-loved?

THE NEED TO REMEMBER

There can be many reasons. But the first is that we often just don't *think* about what we know. We let our awareness of Jesus and of God drop down below the horizon of our conscious world, and we respond to the emptiness we see as if there were nothing more than this to respond to. We are like someone pacing back and forth in an empty apartment instead of sitting down and writing a long, delightful letter to a friend. To write to a friend is to be conscious of that friend. It is to have in one's active memory a face, a smile, an imagined but predictable reaction. It is to hear words, the familiar expressions our friend uses. It is to see and relive again particular moments we have laughed or cried through together. To write to a friend a letter full of memories, or a letter full of news about the present which can only be written to this person in this way because of what we have shared in the past, this is to make the past alive again and the present more alive. It is to make our friend present to what we are now, to what we are feeling and thinking, and to sense with sure knowledge how our friend would respond to all this.

Most letters don't really need an answer. We know what our friend is going to say before we even put our own letter in the mail. It is nice to receive an answer, of course, but usually it just says to us what we have already been anticipating with pleasure that it would say. This is what friends are: people we know well enough to be able to predict — and to count on — their response.

Sometimes, of course, a friend says something we didn't expect; or we did and we didn't. Our friend says the *kind* of thing we expected, the thing that produces the result we hoped for, but says it with a delicacy, or a clarity of insight, or with a particular tenderness that we were not prepared for. That is what makes friendship so beautiful: it is a repeated experience of the old becoming new, of unity flourishing in variety, of recognizing the familiar in the unexpected. It is what St. Augustine said about God: "O beauty ever ancient, ever new!" And St. Paul said the same about Jesus: "Jesus Christ, yesterday, today and the same forever!"

Friendship with Jesus is like this. The reason He is not more of a comfort to us is that we do not allow our thoughts and our imaginations to make Him present. We do not relive with Him memories of things we saw Him do, or are able to see Him do just by closing our eyes and opening our imaginations to the scenes of the Gospels. We don't just sit in His presence, aware of our feelings and our thoughts, allowing Him time to communicate with us.

This is called prayer, of course, but I'd rather not call it that. "Prayer" sounds formal and religious. We are talking about friendship and love. We are talking about remembering, imagining, dreaming, being present in mind and heart to One who actually is present to us and only needs our awareness in order for His presence to become contact.

This is the key to it: awareness. The fact is we have a friend.

The fact is that He is real. And He is present. But we forget about Him. Much — too much — of the time, we think and we act as if He did not exist. No wonder we so often *feel* as if He did not exist. We forget about Him ninety percent of the time, and then when we need Him we want Him to stand out in living color. It just doesn't work like that.

EVERY FRIENDSHIP TAKES TIME

Friendship with Jesus is real, and it can be experienced as strongly as any other friendship. The fact that Jesus cannot be directly seen and touched, or heard with our physical ears when He speaks to us, is not the real problem. The problem is that we will not do the things that let Him be present to us in the way He can be and chooses to be present. And this is a second reason why we don't experience our friendship with Jesus; we will not give to Him the same *time* we give to being present to our other friends. We expect real, experienced friendship with Jesus to happen without any investment of time, although friendship never happens like this. Not with anybody.

Real friendships take time. They take lots of communication. They take lots of living through things together. They require mutual observation — call it contemplation — of each other. They can survive a great deal of physical separation — even an absent friend or lover is a comfort, an enhancement to one's life — but they cannot survive forgetfulness. It is not "out of sight" that makes a friendship fade but "out of mind."

Brother David Stendl-Rast, a Benedictine monk, once said, "The difference between loneliness and solitude is communion." Those who are in communion with others are not alienated, not isolated, not alone. They may be living as hermits, in solitude, as Brother David does much of the year. But their solitude is not loneliness.

To live in conscious, enjoyed communion with Jesus, three things are required, and all three are ours for the choosing. They are *communion of mind, communion of will*, and *communion of heart*. These three means to conscious, enjoyed, experienced friendship with Jesus Christ will be the topics of our next five chapters.

SUMMING UP:

✓ Do you believe it is possible to have with Jesus Christ right now — in your life on earth today — a relationship of love that is as *real* as marriage? As *satisfying* as marriage? As *developmental* of you as a loving person as the most ideal marriage would be?

✓ If you have trouble believing this, reflect on it. Isn't this what Christianity proclaims? Doesn't the life of celibates in the Church bear witness that this love is possible and available — not only to people who vow celibacy, but to all Christians?

✓ Do you experience — do you know — that Jesus is your closest, most intimate, most reliable friend? What is He for you?

✓ How much do you think about Jesus during the day? When, how often, do you talk to Him? About what?

✓ How much time do you give to communicating with Jesus? Is it a regular time? When do you communicate with your other friends?

HELPS TO REFLECT ON THIS CHAPTER: A NEW PRAYER FORM

The first method of meditation we learned (see Chapter One) made use of the three adult powers of communication: *memory, intellect,* and *will.* Now we will practice a new method which is essentially use of the imagination. In the vocabulary of St. Ignatius of Loyola, this method of prayer is called "contemplation."

The first three steps ("vestibule") to enter into prayer are the same ones we have used all along: recall the presence of God, acknowledge it with some physical gesture, and ask God to help you enter into deep, personal communication with Him through prayer.

The next step is to read or recall some scene from the life of Jesus in the Gospels. Or you might place yourself in any other imaginative setting with Jesus: see Him sitting on your bed in your room, or imagine yourself meeting Him on the road somewhere in Galilee, or just sit down and have coffee with Him. The point is to get into a setting or scene in your imagination which allows you to interact with Jesus.

(*Note*: When you imagine the scene, see it in your imagination the way you see things around you with your senses in real life. Don't be distracted by details. At this very moment you are not conscious of all the physical details of the room you are in. Unless it is a room you are already familiar with, you probably could not close your eyes and remember even what the ceiling looks like, or what is on the wall behind you! When we are present to a scene in real life, usually our attention is focused on one or two details: someone's face, words we are hearing, music in the background, etc. The point of imaginative prayer is not to design a whole set, as if for a stage play. The point is to *be present* in your imagination to a scene that includes Jesus, and to interact with Him in your imagination just the way you would in real life.)

When you are present to the scene in your imagination, interact with Jesus in the way that comes naturally to you. Be spontaneous. Just let it happen. Say to Him what comes to your mind. Do what you feel moved to do. Hear Him answer you and see Him respond in the way that just seems to happen. Don't try to exercise control or to make up a script. Just be there as if you were daydreaming and let the action unfold on its own.

If nothing happens, if you are just blank, then prime the pump a little. *See* the scene. In your imagination, look at what is there. See if any detail in particular catches your eye. (If it does, focus on that and see what develops.) See the people who are there. See what they are doing. And respond spontaneously.

If that doesn't get you started, or if your attention wanders, then come back by *listening* to what the people there are saying. Let your imagination put words on their lips — the words that occur spontaneously to you; the words you spontaneously think they would be saying or find yourself hearing them say.

If that doesn't work, or if it runs out, then try being conscious of your *feelings* as you listen and see. What are the reactions of your heart? What do you feel Jesus is feeling? What do you sense that other people there are feeling?

The key to this kind of prayer is spontaneity. Don't exercise control. Let the interaction develop freely and take you where it will. This doesn't mean you are completely passive, however. When you feel like saying something to Jesus, then in your imagination say it. And see how He responds. If you feel like doing something, then in your imagination do it. Interact with Jesus. Act and see how He acts in response.

When you are ready to end your prayer, talk to Jesus in your own words. Or to the Father, or the Holy Spirit. Or to Mary, or any of the other saints with whom you may have interacted during your prayer. And if you desire, close with one of the inspired scriptural prayers like the *Our Father* or *Hail Mary*, conscious of the added meaning the words have for you in the light of the prayer you have just made.

SOME SCRIPTURE PASSAGES YOU CAN USE FOR THIS KIND OF PRAYER

You can use this kind of prayer on any passage from Scripture that you are able to visualize and be present to in your imagination. But just to help you get started, here are a few suggestions divided according to the kind of relationship you feel most in need of experiencing with Jesus at this particular time.

Basic Encounter, Inspiration:
- √ Matthew 4:18-22 (call of the disciples)
- √ Matthew 5:1-16 (ideals, Jesus as teacher)
- √ Matthew 8:18-22 (the challenge of following Jesus)
- √ Matthew 9:9-13 (the call of Levi the outsider)
- √ Matthew 9:25-27 (Christ's need for us; what we can do)

Forgiveness, Healing:
- √ Matthew 8:1-4 (cure of the leper)
- √ Matthew 8:5-13 (cure of the centurion's servant)
- √ Matthew 9:1-8 (forgiveness and cure of a paralytic)
- √ Matthew 9:18-26 (cure of an embarrassed woman; restoring life)
- √ Matthew 9:27-31 (cure of two blind men who called)

Strengthening, Trust:
- √ Matthew 8:23-27 (the storm on the lake)
- √ Matthew 8:28-34 (Jesus overcomes the devil)

CHAPTER TEN

To Be In Communion Of Mind With Jesus

(Who is He for you?)

IT IS A wonderful thing to be in communion of mind with someone — to know that we are not alone with our thoughts, our beliefs, our way of looking at things, our convictions about life and about the things that are important to us. We like to share our insights, the understanding we have acquired through our experiences. Even if a friend does not agree with everything we think, we still find it an enormous consolation to have someone who knows, someone who understands what is within us and what means so much to us. And where there is agreement, where there is union of minds, the communion is that much more intense, that much more satisfying. Then friendship is the blessing of all blessings.

More: there is something extraordinarily comforting — I almost said "relieving" — about having someone, a friend, who also wants to share every thought, every feeling with us. We are all by nature such strangers to one another, each so enclosed in a separate, private, and isolating shell of personal existence, that we experience something like rejection, or at least a lack of total acceptance, from everyone who does not choose to be, does not want to be, completely open and revealed to us. We feel held at a distance.

I am not saying that we suffer very intensely, or even consciously at all, from the fact that the population at large are not dying to tell us all their personal secrets! I mean that the fact of this very natural, and I suppose normal, reserve existing between people just makes us ache in a deep way for at least one relationship in which there will be no barriers, no reserves, no holding back, no refusal of self-revelation, sharing, and intimacy. We would like to feel and to know that there is at least one person in this world who wants to know us and be known completely by us; who values us enough to want to be one with us in this unlimited way. We feel the need for this. We feel a need to be paired with someone in a complete sharing of ourselves. One human existence by itself is an inadequacy; two human existences, shared unreservedly, are an experience of fulfillment.

But to enter into this experience we have to find someone who wants to share everything with us: someone whose burning desire is to know us and be known by us without any reserves at all. Such a person is available to us in Jesus Christ.

IN JESUS, GOD IS KNOWABLE

By nature God is unknowable to us. Although we can discover a certain number of things *about* God from examining the universe He made, we cannot actually *know* God unless He reveals Himself to us person-to-person. And there is all the difference in the world between knowing *about* God and *knowing* God. I know something about the engineer who designed the computer I am writing on, because to design this machine took someone pretty smart. An archeologist, digging this computer out of the ruins ten thousand years from now, could perhaps know from the history of technology that the designing engineer had to have lived in the twentieth century. But neither I nor the archeologist could claim to actually know that engineer. Not as a person. The same is true of the God whom we can discover through examining the things He made.

In Jesus, however, God has drawn near. In Jesus, God has taken flesh as a human being. And He did this precisely so that we might know Him. He lived among us, experiencing the world in a human way, responding to it in a human way, expressing His response in a human way. He saw and felt and

106

tasted things just as we do. He grasped the meaning of the world in human thoughts. He reacted to the people around Him with human feelings. And He expressed His feelings and His responses in human words, human actions, human gestures. It's all there in the Gospels, described in human language for us to translate back into living color through our imaginations so that we can see, hear, and feel for ourselves what we would have seen, heard, and felt if we had been physically present to Jesus in His own time and space.

WE NEED TO INVEST THE HUMAN EFFORT

All this is ours for the asking. All we have to do is give to communication with Jesus the time we would give to communicating with anyone else we desired to be close to. If we want to understand His thoughts, to be united with Him in mind, to be a friend who thinks as He does, looks upon life and death and the world as He does, shares His attitudes toward the things of this world, toward other people, toward God — and toward the value of our own existence — then all we have to do is invest the time in becoming one in mind with Him that we would invest in becoming one in mind with anyone else we wanted to be friends with.

Friendship with Jesus, union of mind with Jesus, is not something difficult, or reserved for a select few. It is not something that only those in a particular lifestyle or set of circumstances can aspire to — like monks or nuns, for example, or people who lead lives free from the distractions of our busy world (are there such people?). Friendship with Jesus is available to anyone who wants it enough to give the time to communicating with Him that any friendship requires. Friendship with Jesus costs — initially, at least — exactly what any other friendship costs. And, just as in any friendship, what we get out of it will depend on how much we put into it. It is up to us to decide whether we want to be just friends with Jesus, or close friends, or intimate, or totally united with Him in mind and will and heart — just as it is up to us to decide how close we want to be with anyone else who offers us love. No special call is necessary beyond the call of baptism itself; no special gift of prayer, no special qualities of body or soul, no special traits of character. All we need is faith, desire, and a decision.

The first step in this decision is to give some *time* to understanding Jesus. Jesus expressed Himself in human words and actions, just as the rest of us do. If we want to understand Him, therefore, we have to *think about* what He said and what He did.

This means we simply sit down one day and start taking the Gospels seriously. We start by reading the account of some incident in Jesus' life: the story of His birth, for example, or the description of how He responded to someone who asked Him for help. We read that story the way we would listen to something someone told us about a friend, or about someone we wanted to get to know as a friend. We ask ourselves as we read, "What kind of man is this? How does He think? What did He mean when He said this? Why did He respond in this particular way? How would He respond to me if I approached Him in the same way? How *does* He respond to me?"

There is nothing very complicated about it. You don't have to be a genius to do it, or a saint. You just have to want to know Jesus — want it enough to give some time to it. Want it enough to think about what He said and did. Want it enough to take Him seriously, and to take seriously His human life on earth.

A PRACTICE RUN

Let's take a look at how this is done in practice.

We want to take something Jesus said and think about it until we can say we are truly one in mind with Him on this particular issue. Let's begin with something rather challenging. Let's take the passage in Matthew's Gospel in which Jesus reveals His game plan, His strategy for renewing society and bringing human life on earth up to the level it should be on. This is found in chapter sixteen of Matthew, verses thirteen to twenty-eight. The first thing we want to do is read the passage attentively. So do that now, before going any further in this book.

Did you read the passage? All right, now let's use our intellects to take seriously what Jesus says here, and to try to become one in mind with Him about the way He should save the world. To begin with, we should note that the passage we are considering doesn't appear until we are more than halfway through the Gospel. In other words, this is something Jesus didn't reveal right away, even to His closest friends. It is something He took a long time preparing them to hear, and when He did tell them His plan they could not accept it. So we should not expect that it will be easy for us to agree with Him either. In other words, for our practice run on trying to become one in mind with Jesus by reflecting on His words, we have chosen one of the hardest things in the Gospel to agree with. No one can accuse us of trying to make things look easier than they are!

To prepare ourselves to accept what He says, we have to remember that the words of Jesus are the words of God Himself, and that the mind they reveal to us, although it is the human mind of Jesus, is nevertheless the mind of the infinite, divine Second Person of the Blessed Trinity, God the Son. It would be strange if we found ourselves able, right off the bat, to understand and accept everything Jesus teaches. That would put us on the level of the Teacher before we had even gone through the learning process. So let's approach this passage expecting to find it a challenge.

First of all, let's ask the question, "How does Jesus introduce what He is going to say here? How does He lead into it?"

He begins by asking His disciples, "Who do the people think I am? What are they saying about me out there?"

They answer that some of the people just take Him to be a prophet. This is pretty good, of course, but it is far from what Jesus really was or claimed to be. The Muslims accept Jesus as a prophet, and many people in our culture who do not claim to be Christians would accept Jesus as a wise man with many prophetic insights into truth and values. But Jesus knows that before people can accept the real depth and mystery of what He came to teach, they will have to see Him as something more than just another enlightened — even divinely enlightened — human being.

The disciples tell Him that some of the people do believe He is more than just an ordinary prophet! He is one of the greats from the past — one of the greatest, in fact — come back to life again: like Elijah or Jeremiah. (The disciples made this same mistake again later — they were slow learners — when they saw Jesus transfigured on the mountain, standing with Moses and Elijah. Peter, thinking He was paying Jesus a compliment, suggested they put up a shrine on the mountaintop with three niches: one for Moses, one for Elijah, and one for Jesus. It blew Peter's mind to think that Jesus was one of the Big Three, ranking along with Moses, through whom God gave the Law, and with Elijah, who represented all the prophets. As we know, the Father's response to that suggestion flattened the apostles in fear. See Matthew, chapter seventeen, verses one to eight.)

Finally, some of the people were speculating that Jesus was John the Baptizer risen from the dead. In other words, the people knew He was someone great, but they didn't know how great He was or who He really was.

Before going any further, Jesus makes the disciples declare themselves. He asks them that question which, sooner or later, He asks us all: "Who do *you* say that I am?" It is not enough for us to just echo what other people say about Jesus, or to be willing to take their word for it. It is not enough for us even to repeat faithfully what the Church teaches about Him, complacently assuming that because we know what the Church says about Jesus — and after all, we are the Church — we must know Him and accept Him for ourselves. This is a wrong assumption. Jesus doesn't ask, "What does the Church say about me?" — important as that is. He asks, "*Who do you say* that I am?" Each one of us has to take a stand, deeply and personally, toward the identity of Jesus. We have to take this stand in an act of decision for which we take full responsibility. It has to be our judgment about who He is, our decision to accept Him, and our definitive position. "Who do you say that I am? How do you accept me for yourself? What faith do you put in me, and what do you want me to be for you?" Before Jesus can reveal anything more to His disciples (and He deals with us in the same way), He has to make sure that they have made up their minds about Him; that they have accepted Him definitely and irrevocably for what He is.

A PAUSE FOR DECISION

Let's interrupt our reflection on the Gospel at this point. To do so will teach us a valuable lesson about prayer.

The lesson is that we should never try to finish a line of thought we have begun in prayer if something else comes up during it that we feel we have to respond to. For example, we began reflecting on Jesus' game plan, His strategy for delivering human life on earth from the power of evil. But before we even got to what this stategy is, we were faced with another question: "Who do you say that I am?" We saw that before we can expect to believe *what* Jesus says, we first have to believe *who* He is. We have to be sure we believe in Him before we can hope to believe in what He says. This is because some of the things Jesus teaches are simply beyond the range of human reason and we can only accept them by taking His word for it. They never go *against* human reason, but they come from a level of understanding that human reason cannot reach, either for input or for verification. And so, before we can really accept to be guided by Jesus in the orientation we give to our lives, we have to decide once and for all that we will accept the input He provides rather than restrict our judgments to the data we can verify for ourselves. Basically, this means we decide to follow His guidance system rather than our own.

Have we done this? Whether we have or have not, this is a point in prayer at which we should stop our reflection for a moment in order to take a stance with our wills. We want to stop thinking and start choosing; stop just reflecting with our intellects and start responding with our wills, with an act of free and deliberate decision.

"Who do you say that I am?" When Jesus asks this question, He is not asking for an academic, intellectual opinion. He is asking about your free choice, your personal, voluntary decision to believe in Him or not. He wants to know just what you have decided, what you have chosen to believe about Him. Who is He for you? How far will you trust Him? How unconditionally will you follow Him? What is the response to Him that you are willing to base your life on?

This is a question that might call for more reflection. But essentially it calls for a decision. If you have not made that decision already in a deep, deliberate, conscious, and explicit way, now is the time to stop and think about it until you can. It might take a few hours. Or days. But it is the most important decision anyone is called upon to make in life, and everyone must make it sooner or later. Who is Jesus for you? Who do *you* say that He is?

Is He your Savior? Is He just the Savior who gets you to heaven, or is He the Savior — the only Savior — who makes it possible for your life on earth here and now to be what it should be, what you yourself want it to be? Do you believe that anything in your life, any activity or occupation, can be saved from going awry without His being a part of it? Can anything you do without interacting with Him be saved from destructiveness? From distortion? From meaninglessness? From mediocrity?

Is Jesus the Teacher of Life for you? Not just the teacher of "religion" in some restricted sense, but the practical guide whose teachings you study and try to apply creatively to everything you do?

Do you base your family life on His teachings? How? In what ways is your family life different from American family life in general because of specific things you have seen in the Gospels and applied to your lifestyle at home? Do you base your professional life on insights and guidelines you have received from reflecting on the Scriptures? (If you are still in school, do you base your life and choices as a student on principles you have personally discovered in the Gospels?) How is your social life different because you have brought it under the light of Christ's teachings? If in any area of your life — personal life, social life, family life, student or professional life, civic life — you chart your course and make your day-to-day decisions without reference to the principles and ideals, the teaching and example of Jesus Christ, can you really say that He is the Teacher of Life for you? Judging from the way you actually live your life, who do you say that He is?

What about Jesus as Leader? Do you believe He has asked you to work with Him to bring His salvation — His light, His love, His life — to the world? Do you really believe He has called you? If so, what do you do for Him? How do you express your response to Him in your daily choices and decisions? What actions in your life do you identify most clearly as contributions to the life-giving work of Christ? Is there anything you do which does not contribute to His goals? Why?

Is Jesus your friend? How deep a friend? How intimate? Have you accepted Him as your partner in everything you do, in every single act and activity of your life? Can you relate to Him as Spouse? Is He that much a part of your life? Are you committed to seeking perfect union of mind and will and heart with Him, which is the heart and soul of spousal love? Are you pledged to total surrender to Him? To total dedication of all you are to all that He desires? Who is Jesus for you? What do you choose Him to be?

If you have already accepted Jesus, perhaps even years ago, as Savior, as Teacher, as Leader, as Friend, as everything else He wants to be for you, then this is a good time to just rest consciously for a while in the awareness and enjoyment of your relationship with Him. Reaffirm it. Let your will go out to it again. Be conscious of it, and of how good it is for you: how good it has been for you in your life since you accepted Him in these ways. Look at what Jesus is for you and what you are for

Him and be satisfied — the way you would look at something you just built or bought — be glad in it. Rejoice in it and reaffirm it. Reconfirm it. Do this for as long as it takes to come to a sense of completeness, a sense of satisfaction and of peace in the stance that you have taken toward Him. Just be there, glad of what He is for you and you for Him.

This part of your prayer, once your decision about Christ is made and you are able to rest in it contentedly, can also be called "contemplation." (This is not the same as the prayer form we learned at the end of Chapter Nine.) The word, the name you give to it is not important in itself, but it will help you make the connection with your own experience when you read about contemplation somewhere else. Contemplation sounds like an activity of the mind — and, in fact, the mind is active in the sense of being consciously aware of something. But contemplation is really more of an activity of the will than of the mind. It is a loving response to a truth that is believed. The believing and the loving are both an enduring stance of the will. In contemplation they become an experience of the heart.

TIME TO DO THREE THINGS

To arrive at union of mind with Jesus Christ, then, we need to do essentially one thing, which initially divides into three things.

Essentially, we just need to dedicate the *time* to communicating with Him that we would dedicate to getting to know any other person we choose to be friends with. But since communicating with Jesus does not seem to us — until we are used to it, at least — to be as easy as communicating with other people, we have to spell out the particular steps this process involves. (They are the same as the steps involved in communicating with anyone else, but just as we can't tie our shoes deliberately and consciously without thinking it through step by step, in the same way we might have trouble deliberating communicating with Jesus unless we go through it consciously, step by step.)

The steps involved in communicating with Jesus are as follows:

√ First, we have to *be present* to something Jesus said or did. This means we have to stop and notice it, take it seriously, confront its meaning for our lives, and let its meaning confront us. Instead of just taking for granted that Jesus said this and did that, letting the words of the Scripture roll over our minds like treadless tires that don't even leave a track, we stop and focus in on something, asking what significance it ought to have for us. This is step one.

√ Step two is to *ask questions and try to answer them*. These are not abstract, academic questions, but the kind of questions that lead us to take a stance with our wills and to make decisions in response to the message of Jesus. For example, in the passage we have been practicing on, Jesus Himself asks His disciples (and therefore us) a question which we cannot answer until we decide what we are going to base our very lives on: "Who do you say that I am?" This is not an abstract question. To answer with detached intellectuality, "Oh, you are the Second Person of the Blessed Trinity, the Word of God made flesh to be the Savior of the world," is not to answer the question. The question is, "Who do you say I am *for you*? What place are you going to give me in your life?"

Before you can answer this question, you may have to ask a lot of other questions, such as: "What do I really believe about Jesus? What experiences have I had that tell me who He is or what He can be for me? If I don't base my life on responding to Jesus Christ, what will I base it on? What have I been basing it on up to now? I mean, what above all has determined my basic decisions in life? And what have I gained from this? What have I lost? What have I learned from all the decisions I have made, good and bad? What are my highest values now? Where did they come from? How would they change if I decided to base every decision for the rest of my life on the teaching and example of Jesus Christ? How could I go about beginning this?"

All these are obviously questions it could take some time to

115

answer. It may be that you have answered a lot of them already. But the point is that all of them are *real* questions. They all lead to action. They all call for a deep, deliberate, free stance of the will toward Jesus Christ. They are all questions that involve our lives. Step two is to think about a truth until we are ready to act on it.

√ The third step is to *make a decision*. Union of mind with another person is not truly real — or it is insignificant — if it does not involve union of wills. I don't really agree with another person's view of life unless I am willing to live by it — or at least to try. I don't truly accept another person's priorities unless I am trying to make them my own. To be truly one in mind with Jesus means that I have the courage to say, "This is what I believe in, this is what I will base my life on." It means to put belief into action.

Try to take this stance toward Jesus Christ. If you have not already done so, try to decide — deeply, firmly, and personally — that for the rest of your life you will look first of all to the teaching and example of Jesus Christ for the standard, the criterion by which to make every judgment and decision you will make from now on. Decide to place all your hope in Him — not only to look to Him for all the help, all the security you need for the future, but also to identify fulfillment and happiness in life with being one in mind and will and heart with him. Try to decide once and for all, as St. Paul did and urges us to do, that to live just means to love and serve Jesus Christ, and everything else is insignificant compared to that (see Paul's Letter to the Philippians, especially chapter one, verses twenty-one and twenty-two, and chapter three, verses seven to fifteen).

If you have already made this decision, rest in it and let it absorb your soul.

TO HELP YOU RESPOND TO THIS CHAPTER:

The essential response to this chapter is just to answer the question "Who do you say that I am?" To do this it would be good to take up the specific titles proposed earlier in the chapter: Is Jesus Savior for you? Teacher? Leader? Friend? Spouse? And you can add any other titles of your own or seek the title that best describes what Jesus is for you and what you want Him to be for you right now at this point in your life.

To help you through the process of deciding who Jesus is for you, you might want to begin with the three questions below:

✓ 1. Do I want to take Jesus seriously enough to give time to thinking about what He said and did during His human life on earth?

✓ 2. Am I willing to read and reflect on the Gospels in order to understand better the mind and heart of Christ? When during the day will I do this? How often? (Every day?) Where? For how long each time?

✓ 3. Am I ready now to answer the question "Who is Jesus Christ for me?" If not, am I ready to make a deliberate, conscious decision to keep dealing with this question until I can answer it? How, concretely, will I go about answering it?

Reflect on these questions, using the *method of meditation* explained at the end of Chapter One. Save some of your prayer time at the end to review and absorb your prayer, using the *Prayer Enhancer* described at the end of Chapter Four.

CHAPTER ELEVEN

Understanding And Accepting The Strategy Of Jesus

WE STILL haven't seen what the strategy of Jesus is for redeeming the quality of human life on earth.

The disciples had one job description in their minds for the Messiah. It came out of the Scriptures according to the way everyone interpreted them at the time. If Jesus had told them from the beginning what He was going to do to save the world, they would have decided that He did not match the job description of the Savior they all expected, and they would have rejected Him. So He didn't tell them *how* He was going to save the world until they accepted Him unconditionally as the one who was going to do it.

In answer to His question, however, "Who do you say that I am?" Peter responds unconditionally and definitively in the name of all: "You are the Christ, the Messiah, the Son of the living God."

This is what Jesus has been waiting for. Now that they have accepted Him as the Savior, with no more questioning or turning back, He can tell them how He is going to save the world. It won't be what they expected.

In a nutshell, what He tells them is: "I am going to save the world from evil by enduring evil with love."

WHAT IS "SALVATION"?

We are talking here about Jesus' strategy for restoring and elevating the quality of human life on earth. As Savior, Jesus came to do two things. First, and essentially, He came to take away — to annihilate — all the sins we would ever commit. He did this by taking into His own Body the sins of every member of the human race who would be incorporated into His Body through baptism,* and by carrying those sins into annihilation through His death on the cross. The true salvation of the world is a mystery of our dying and rising again in Christ, a mystery of people being granted a share in the divine life of God through the grace of incorporation into the Body and life of Jesus Christ. This is what takes away the sins of the world.*

But the salvation of the world also includes the means Jesus uses to redeem, to restore, and to renew the attitudes, values, and patterns of behavior that determine the quality of human life on earth. Jesus came to deliver us from the domination and effects of sin in this world, and to make human life on earth what it is truly called to be. He came, not just to get us to heaven, but to establish His kingship on earth, to overcome evil within this world. His strategy for overcoming evil in this world is simply to endure it with love. That is what we cannot accept.

What Jesus told His disciples was that He was going to overcome evil by letting evil have its way with Him; by allowing Himself to be arrested, unjustly condemned, tortured, and put to death. And all those who desire to follow Jesus must agree to overcome evil in the same way — by accepting any suffering or injustice that comes to them and enduring it with love. This is what it means to "carry one's cross" with Jesus. It means to respond with love to that portion of the consequences of the sin of the world, whatever it might be, which happens to fall on one's own particular shoulders.

This doesn't sound like deliverance from evil; it sounds like deliverance *to* evil! If the best the Savior can do is tell us to en-

---

* This includes the sins of those saved by baptism of desire, of course. For an explanation, see my book *Why Jesus?* (available through His Way Communications, 1310 Dellwood, Memphis TN 38127).

dure our pain and suffering with love — to grin and bear it —
He doesn't appear to be much of a savior. The Savior is sup-
posed to deliver us from evil, not abandon us to it. No wonder
Peter objected. No wonder we all do!

WE BECOME LIKE GOD

The key to this is that Jesus does not tell us just to endure
evil. He tells us to endure it *with love*. To take up one's cross
does not mean just to carry it patiently. It means to carry it as
Jesus did, loving those who placed it on Him, offering His pain
that they might come to the fullness of life. Whenever we do this
we are delivered from all evil; we have overcome it.

Think about it. Jesus does not promise to stamp out all evil
action on earth. He could not do that without taking away human freedom. God did not send Jesus to force, or even to manip-
ulate, people into doing what is right all the time. He sent Jesus
to deliver us from evil; to make evil unable to harm us.

Jesus was not sent to clean up the environment, unless in-
directly, through what His followers would do. He was sent to
save people, to make people different, to free people from the de-
stroying, life-diminishing consequences of sin. If Jesus had just
cleaned up the human environment, even by taking all crime
and violence, all the oppression and deceitful manipulation out
of the world, we who live in the world would still be basically
the same. We might not sin as much, but it would be for lack of
temptation, not because we ourselves had become more loving,
enlightened, and strong. We ourselves would not be any closer
to embracing, with deep, interior understanding, the attitudes
and values of God; we would just be subjected to less bad programming from the sinful culture of this world — or to no bad
programming at all — but we would not have chosen truth and
goodness with a clear realization of the alternatives. We would
not have faced sin and overcome it; we would simply have been
spared the confrontation.

Jesus did not come to save the environment — directly, at
least — but to save us. He came to enable us, to empower us, to

become different; in fact, to become like God. Not like God just in the sense that we were created in His image — to be like God in this sense just means that our natures are like His by the fact that we have intellects and wills: we can think; we can understand; we can freely choose. In this we are like God by nature, because we can do what He does — we can know and choose and love — and this is a likeness to God which was simply given to us at creation.

But Jesus came to enable us to be like God as persons: to be like God in what we freely create ourselves to be by our responses, by our choices. He came to enable us to become like God in our freely-adopted attitudes and values, in the self-determining stance that we adopt in mind and will and heart toward everything that is. In a nutshell, He came to enable us to be like God in the most radical, fundamental decision we are called upon to make on this earth, which is the decision, based on faith in His words and example, to lead lives characterized by love.

THE KEY IS LOVE

God is love. One way to define God is to say that He is that Being who freely chooses to love every human being on this earth. We could say God is that Being whose nature it is to do this, but that would make it appear that God is just programmed to love; that it is not a free choice. In reality, God is that Being whose nature it is to be the One who freely chooses to do this. That is, God is that Being whose self-defining characteristic it is to choose to invest everything He is in what we human beings can become (see above, Chapter One). And He is faithful in that. He never gives up on us, never rejects us, never refuses to forgive, never writes us off. Whatever sins we commit against Him, whatever evil we do, His response to us always is to love.

In Jesus, God revealed His love — and revealed His deepest self — by coming into the world, making Himself vulnerable to the same pain and suffering to which we are vulnerable, and loving back in response to everything that was done to Him.

When He was rejected, He loved back; when He was betrayed, He loved back; when He was unjustly condemned, He loved back; when He was tortured, He loved back; when He was crucified and murdered, He loved back. And He taught us that to be followers of His, to enter by free choice into the Life He came to give, to be like God in the way He empowers us to be, we also have to dedicate ourselves to loving without conditions or restraints.

This is the game plan of Jesus. It is His strategy for renewing and saving human life on earth. And it does deliver us from evil. It does not protect us from pain and suffering; Jesus did not promise to do that. But it does protect us from all harm. If we accept the salvation Jesus offers us — the grace to love back in response to everything that is done to us — nothing can harm us.

We have seen this already in Chapters Four and Six. If I am sinned against — robbed, betrayed, rejected, raped, or mutilated — and I choose to become a hater, then, yes, I have been harmed. I have become less good as a person by my response; my life is diminished; I am less like God. But if I respond with love, then everything that is done to me just serves to boost me higher and higher. I become more loving, more truly filled with life, more like God, and more in possession of His own happiness and joy than I was before. If I respond to everything with love, nothing can take my soul from me. Everything will help me to grow.

GOD'S USE OF POWER

This is where the power of Jesus as Savior appears. He refused to use the kind of power we already knew God had: the power to defeat enemies in battle, to kill off the bad guys, to terrify people into submission. But by that very fact He called our attention to another power He has — one much harder to believe in: Jesus has the power as our Savior to enable us to love as God does. He can empower us to love back — to love back, no matter what is done to us. Jesus saves us by enabling us to love.

We would make a great mistake if we thought this meant Jesus enables us to *feel* loving, affectionate, or even forgiving toward those who hurt us. Our salvation has very little to do with feeling, because feelings are not free responses. They are not self-determining actions; they do not determine who we are as persons. Jesus Himself, in His agony in the garden, did not feel like saving the world. He did not feel like sacrificing Himself for us in love. He felt like calling the whole thing off. He felt scared, crushed, discouraged, unwilling to do what the Father asked.

He felt unwilling. But He *was* willing. He felt as though He had no love at all, but He did the most loving thing that has ever been done in the history of the world. And He calls us, His followers, not to *feel* love and forgiveness for one another, but simply to love and to forgive.

This is Jesus' strategy for saving the world. Do we — do we choose to — accept it? Since this chapter is an exercise in seeking union of mind with Jesus, we need to think about this proposition of His until we can at least understand His reasons for it. We need to weigh the alternatives in our minds: loving back in response to evil vs. fighting back, retaliating, hating.

We need to call upon our memories: to look back in history — even into the history of our own short lives — and ask what the long-range effects of retaliation have been. Has the policy of retaliation, which the human race has followed since history began, succeeded in bringing peace to the world? Have we ever found peace ourselves — real peace — by getting back at someone?

(*Note:* Don't confuse "getting back at" someone with *letting someone know* what you think or feel about something done to you. It can be hard to live with an unspoken truth. Communication — speaking the truth to someone — is often essential for peace of mind. But there is nothing unloving about speaking the truth. On the contrary, *not* to speak the truth, not to tell someone that we are offended or hurt when we are, can be very unloving. God is not guilty of this: he tells us very clearly what pleases Him and what offends Him. And if we do anything wrong, He lets us know so that we can face it and decide what we want to do about it. If we think that we have sometimes found peace through retaliation, we should ask what gave us the peace: punishing or getting back at those who hurt us, or just letting them know how we felt about it.)

BEING ONE MIND WITH CHRIST

Here, then, is a teaching of Jesus to wrestle with. Don't expect to find it easy to accept. If it does seem easy, test yourself by imagining different situations in which you could be called upon to forgive terrible injustices and see if you find it credible that you could love back — or at least that you *should* love back. When it comes to the teaching of Jesus, the only true test of our acceptance is the response we are willing to make in action. The effort we make to put His teaching into practice is the measure of what we believe.

So put your mind to work on the plan Jesus has for the redemption of human life on earth. Look at it from every angle. Match it up against your experience. Test it for practicality. Apply it to concrete examples in your own life: past, present, or imagined. Take it out of the clouds and bounce it off the down-to-earth experience you have of living at ground level. Argue with Jesus, then ask yourself how you think He would argue back. And see if at the end of all this you know that your attitude toward what is needed to lift up the quality of human life in this world is more in conformity with His.

QUESTIONS TO HELP YOU REFLECT ON THIS CHAPTER

✓ 1. Read Matthew 16:21-28. Do you understand what Jesus is saying here? How could you rephrase and put into your own words the strategy Jesus announces here for delivering the world from evil?

✓ 2. Do you accept the call of Jesus to endure evil with

love? To love back in response to all that is done to you? What reasons can you give in favor of what Jesus teaches here? (*Note*: This does not mean we do not try to prevent evil, or to restrain people who would do evil things. It simply tells us the attitude of heart we should take, and that in turn will guide us to the best response we can make when evil is done.)

√ 3. Reflect on some experience in your life when you were deeply hurt by someone, or when you were the victim of real injustice. Did you respond to this with love? If not, what were the results of your response? Can you respond to the event or the person now with love? What would this mean, concretely? How do you feel about this in the light of what Jesus teaches here?

Reflect on these questions, using the *method of meditation* explained at the end of Chapter One. Save some prayer time at the end to review and absorb your prayer, using the *Prayer Enhancer* described at the end of Chapter Four or the *Review Questions* based on the gifts of the Holy Spirit which are given at the end of Chapter Five.

CHAPTER TWELVE

Union Of Will With Jesus

THERE IS NO true union of mind without union of wills. We do not really agree with another's attitude toward life until we are ready to adopt it as the working attitude of our own life. Until we see it clearly and vividly enough to choose it, we don't see it clearly enough to be of one mind with our friend about it.

Seeing and choosing, however, are two different things, and their relationship with each other can be subtle. Just the fact that I am unwilling to choose something can be enough to keep me from seeing it. When we say that something "doesn't make sense" to us, we often mean that it just doesn't appeal to us. We truly don't see it clearly enough to choose it, but the reason we don't see it is that, deep down, we don't want to choose it.

This means that, even while we work at becoming one in mind with Jesus, we have to work at becoming one with Him in what we desire.

It is a significant fact that, when His disciples asked Jesus to teach them how to pray, He responded by giving them a list of priorities they should make their own. They were, in fact, the priorities of His own heart.

"When you pray, say: 'Father!:

— may Your name — may You — be hallowed, loved, respected . . .

— may Your kingdom come . . .

— may Your will be done on earth as it is in heaven . . .

— give us this day our daily bread . . .

— and forgive us our offenses, as we also forgive . . .

— do not allow us to come into hard testing . . .

— but deliver us from evil.' "

PRIORITIES ENABLE PRAYER

Jesus did not really teach His disciples to pray by giving them a formula of words to memorize and recite. There is proof enough of this in the fact that the wording of what we call the Lord's Prayer is slightly different in the different Gospels. (Compare, for example, Matthew 6:9-13 and Luke 11:2-4.) That is enough to show that the disciples were not concentrating on getting the words exactly right. But the content and order of the petitions which make up this prayer are basically the same. This shows that what Jesus is teaching here is the priority of desires that should rule our hearts. If we want easy familiarity with God in prayer, the way to get there is to restructure our desires.

Facility in prayer, intimacy with God, does not come from finding the right method of prayer or from mastering the right technique. I do not say that these are unimportant. It is just that Jesus did not teach His disciples a method of prayer; He taught them purity (single-mindedness) of heart. He did not teach them how to focus their minds; He taught them where to focus their desires.

The Lord's Prayer is really just a revelation of Christ's own heart. "If you want to pray like me," He tells us, "desire like me."

Then He tells us the desires that rule His life.

THE DESIRES OF JESUS

When Jesus was on earth, what He desired above all else, what He lived and breathed for, was that the Father should be known and loved, that the Father's name should mean to every person on earth what it meant to Him. This was the desire which, above all others, determined and motivated every choice He made.

His second desire was that God's kingship, His rule, should be established over every human heart, over every area and activity of human life. This is what Jesus lived and worked and died for.

Then He desired that the Father's will should be done in everything, on earth as perfectly as it is in heaven. On the feeling level He did not always desire this, as He showed in the garden before His passion. But even then the desire of His will was constant: "Not my will, but yours be done." Regardless of His feelings, He knew that His own good — and all good — was to be found in the will of the Father.

After this came trust in the Father for everything He would need, a trust that asked only what was necessary for the moment — "give us this day our daily bread" — without insisting on visible reserves to rely upon. (Actually, according to the probable meaning of the Greek words, the real focus of this petition is not on "daily" bread, but on the "future" bread of the heavenly banquet, the bread of the wedding feast, which was our Lord's way of describing the eternal celebration of heaven. See Raymond Brown, "The Lord's Prayer as an Eschatological Prayer," in *New Testament Essays* [Doubleday].)

Jesus had no need to ask forgiveness for Himself. But the desire of His heart was that every human person should be reconciled to the Father and to every other. And so He taught us to echo His own desire that the Father's forgiveness would be accepted, and that we would all forgive one another. He taught us to pray, not for revenge, or even for justice in the punishment of sinners, but for what He Himself lived and worked for; that forgiveness might overcome sin. "Forgive us . . . as we also forgive. . ."

In the second-to-last petition Jesus reveals His trust in the Father not to let Him be tested beyond His strength, and at the same time expresses His reliance on the Father to determine just how far He will allow that testing to go. Jesus really wanted the limits of what He would be asked to give to be set, not by Himself, but by the Father. His desire was to be in the Father's hands completely. As His Mother expressed it before Him, "Let it be done to me according to your word."

Finally, Jesus longed for the day when the world would be definitively "delivered from evil." He wanted the Father's victory over sin and death, won through His own dying on the cross, to be complete. He didn't insist that the Father should take all evil out of the world immediately, or spare Him from being hit by the consequences of sin upon earth. But He did ask and desire that finally all evil would be overcome and that the triumph of God's love would be complete. And this is what He taught us to work and pray for.

These priorities are a thumbnail sketch of Jesus' heart, a revelation of His deepest desires. Now ask yourself: Are they the first and deepest desires of your own heart?

WHAT ARE YOUR DESIRES?

Don't be too quick to say they are not — especially if you have been taking your religion seriously for many years. Could it be that, when you consult what is really most important for you, you can say that what you desire more than anything else in life is just that God be known, respected, and loved?

And that His kingdom be established? That the whole human race might surrender to His life-giving reign in faith, in hope, and in love?

Have you experienced enough of life already to know that, deep down, you want God's will to be done always, even if it is hard on you at the moment, because in His will is all your good and all the good that anyone can hope for?

Can you say yes to these questions? Do these first three petitions of the *Our Father* express what is in fact your most basic, most constant stance toward life? The deepest desires of your heart?

Again, is your experience of life such that at this point you are willing to rely on God from day to day, without needing to see ahead of time how He is going to provide for you? Do you still need the comforting assurance of surplus money in the bank? Of guaranteed employment? Of friends or family you know you can count on? Do you feel you have to know what God has planned for your future? Or are you content just to take what He provides from day to day — your "daily bread" — and live in quiet trust that His concern for you will never fail?

Have you learned from experience that the bread of this world does not really satisfy? That the only bread that can fill your heart is the bread Jesus came to give — the bread of the heavenly wedding feast?

Are you willing to forgive at last? Does reconciliation with others have more appeal for you now than revenge or retaliation? Would you rather be reconciled to God yourself now than cling to any sin that may have separated you from Him in the past? Have you reached that stage in life where peace and harmony with God and with others take precedence over all lesser values? Where loving, forgiving acceptance among people means more to you than the issues you used to fight about? Do you find your own heart in the prayer "Forgive us . . . as we forgive. . ."?

Have the fears and anxieties of your younger days yielded to a deep abandonment of yourself into the caring hands of God? Do you leave it to God to protect you from being asked to give or to suffer more than you can bear? Do you simply ask Him, "Lead us not into temptation," and then trust Him to preserve you from too hard a testing, without trying to take too much control of the situation yourself? Can you simply leave your future, your security, even your salvation in His hands?

Lastly, do you live in constant desire that all evil should be overcome? Are you less and less indifferent to sin and injustice in the world? Even to those sins and injustices which do not affect you personally? Do you burn, without compulsive violence, to see sin overcome, the wounds of people healed, the true beauty of creation restored, and God's goodness manifest in everything that is? Has "Deliver us from evil" become the aching desire of your soul?

If you find — perhaps to your amazement — that this is a pretty accurate assessment of the priorities of your heart, then rejoice: you are experiencing graced identification with Jesus Christ! Over the years more and more His thoughts have become your thoughts, His ways your ways, His desires your desires. And you can say with St. Paul, "The life I am living, the life I experience now, is not just my own; Christ lives in me!" (see Galatians 2:20).

If these are not your true priorities, don't be discouraged. You just have some growing to do. Your will is not yet completely attuned to Christ's will. (Not that it ever will be *perfectly* one with His will this side of heaven, but we can come close!) You just have to reexamine your desires — your most basic ones, at least — and call some of them into question. You have to restructure your priorities. You have to change your heart.

THE FREEDOM OF DESIRE

This can be done. "Desire," as I am using the word here, is not just a natural appetite, a feeling, a spontaneous inclination, I am speaking about *chosen* desire: desire we don't just recognize within ourselves as a spontaneous inclination, but positively accept with our wills; desire we are willing to give our name to: desire that we welcome as our own. There is all the difference in the world between a desire that comes in uninvited to seduce me and a desire to which I have issued a pass. I can recognize a spontaneous inclination within myself and reject it. That doesn't make it go away — if it did there would be no such thing as persistent temptation — but it makes it an intruder, an alien invader, a squatter within my heart without the right of residence. It means that the desire is just an unmandated reaction of my nature, and not a free response of my person. Such a desire does not create me as a person; it does not give shape to my soul.

There are other desires which may not be spontaneous inclinations at all. In fact, on the feeling level I may experience nothing but rejection of them. And yet they can be the true desires of my heart. These are the desires I choose to have, desires for what I choose to want, the desires of my will. These desires make me what I am as a person. These desires are the shape of my soul.

These are desires I can change. I can look at what I actually want in an active, deliberate sense, and I can decide to keep or to reject these desires. If I keep a desire, this means that I accept its object as something I choose for myself, something I choose to identify as good for me; as an ingredient of the happiness I seek; as contributing to the fulfillment I have targeted for myself.

Take for example two people who smoke, both of whom are addicted. Suppose you are one of them. And suppose that you have really confronted the issue and become convinced that smoking is too dangerous to be acceptable. You may still be smoking, unable to break the habit, but you have decided you really don't want to. So every time you smoke you say to yourself, "This is not what I want for myself; this is stupid!" You continue to bring into your awareness — through reading, conversation, group therapy, or whatever — the bad effects smoking can have on your health. You keep looking for something that will free you and enable you to stop. I would say that in all likelihood sooner or later you will stop. For you, smoking is a compulsion; but it is not a desire you have embraced with your will. You are not really a smoker; you are essentially a nonsmoker who smokes! And you are not happy with what you are doing. You are in conflict. Smoking is not you.

Suppose, on the other hand, that you are the other member of this duo. You may not actually smoke — for the time being — any more than the first person does. But you have not rejected smoking as bad for you. Oh, you may know as much as anyone else about the likelihood of lung cancer terminating your career. But you have decided that smoking is worth the risk for you. You have placed smoking among those things you select to pack into your bag for the journey; things you consider significant for the happiness you have designed in your mind for yourself; things you settle on to be part of your enjoyment of life. When you smoke, you don't say, "This is crazy; I don't want this!" You smoke as an act of fulfilling your desire in life. You are happy to smoke because you have chosen to accept smoking as an ingredient of your happiness. Your physical and psychological longing for a smoke may not be any stronger than the other person's; but your longing has the backing of your will, of your deliberate desire. You don't just smoke; you are a smoker. And you are glad to be one. Smoking is you.

What difference does it make to renounce a desire with your will when you are unable to break a habit or resist a particular temptation in practice? If your compulsion to smoke is so strong that you continue to smoke even after you have chosen interiorly not to desire it, isn't the end result the same? Doesn't this make your choosing or not choosing to desire something just a mental fiction? Doesn't it mean you are kidding yourself?

DIVIDED DESIRE

It might. But if my desire is real, then I as a person am different. My will is truly in union with the will of Christ. I may not be completely in union with His will; I may not be *totally* surrendered; but at least there is something real in me, a part of me, that chooses to want what He wants and desires to desire what He desires. The reason I am not totally surrendered to Christ is that I am not totally in control of myself. I am not completely one with Him because I am not completely one with myself (and vice versa). I can say with St. Paul that there is a struggle for power going on inside me. There is the real me, the freeborn me, who desires what Christ desires. And there is the false me, the slave me, who obeys other voices than my own. And so I wind up sometimes doing, not the good that I love, but the evil that I hate. This is not the real me. (See Romans 7:14-25.)

There is always the possibility of rationalization here, of course. I might go around telling people — and telling myself — that I "really don't want to smoke" when everyone (except me) knows that smoking doesn't bother me at all; that I am quite satisfied to be a smoker. A little honest self-confrontation will take care of this rationalization.

The most likely answer, however, is simply that I am divided. As a person I am not together, not completely in union with myself! I can desire to smoke and desire not to smoke at the same time. I may see its danger for me and want to reject it, but something else in me can keep clinging to the satisfaction or relief that smoking gives me. In this case my desire to stop smoking is real (as real as my desire to *smoke*); it just isn't strong enough.

This is what St. Paul was writing about. From experience. He was keenly aware that he frequently did not do what in his mind he really desired to do, and he did the things that interiorly he had decided not to do. He recognized conflicting forces at war within himself. This is the ordinary human condition — especially when we are sharing in the life of Christ by grace and His Spirit is dwelling within us, working to purify us of sin. In the process of seeking union of will with Jesus, one of the first things we experience is disunion within ourselves. As soon as we set our hearts on peace, we realize we are already at war.

The remedy for this dividedness is motivation: more motivation than I have right now. If I get desperate enough about smoking, for example, or can't stand the interior conflict any longer, or actually get lung cancer, or have a heart attack, my desire to stop smoking may become strong enough to overcome the desire to smoke, and I will actually stop. We frequently come to a decision like this the hard way: when so much pain, suffering, and damage have resulted from what we are doing that we just can't stand it anymore, we finally make up our minds.

This is the hard way, and the tragic way to come to unity of desire. Why do we have to wait until slavery becomes intolerable before we will throw off our chains? This is a tragic way to come to a decision because the cost is so great — to ourselves and to others. But there is another way: it is the way of freedom through love, and it follows the path of *increasing faith* and *persevering prayer*. We will describe this in the following chapter.

SUMMING UP:

✔ The key to praying well is to have the same priorities that God has. Jesus teaches us this is the *Our Father*, which is essentially a revelation of the priorities and desires of His own heart.

✔ As we go through life and grow in the spiritual life, we should find that our own deepest, most constant desires in life have become the same as those expressed by Jesus in the *Our Father*.

✔ Although as *feelings* our desires are not something we can turn on and off at will, nevertheless our true *personal* desires — the desires that characterize us as unique human persons and determine "who" we are — are free. These are the desires we have chosen to accept and to ratify with our wills. It is this level of desire which we express in the *Our Father*.

✔ Most of us are divided in our desire. We want and we don't want what Christ desires. To achieve unity and whole-heartedness, we have to work at embracing all the desires of Christ's heart and rejecting any desires that are not according to His. This can be done.

✔ The best way to do this is not to rely on asceticism — willpower, self-domination — alone, but to work especially through *faith* and *persevering prayer*.

A METHOD OF PRAYER FOR THIS CHAPTER (RHYTHMICAL PRAYER):

I would suggest a combination of methods for prayer over this chapter. Begin by using both the standard method of meditation (confronting a statement, asking questions, making a decision — which is the use of *memory, intellect,* and *will* described at the end of Chapters One and Ten), and the method described at the end of Chapter Six: the *method for praying over prayers* to make all your prayers more personal. You can follow this with what St. Ignatius calls *rhythmical prayer* (described below) in order to unite your heart affectively with the desires of Christ presented in the *Our Father.* In the concrete this means:

√ 1. Begin with the usual "vestibule" of prayer: presence of God, acknowledgement, petition.

√ 2. Take the first petition of the *Our Father*: "Father . . . hallowed be thy name." Confront it, explore its meaning, feel what it means to you, ask what it should mean and could mean, and how you could make it mean more to you personally. Use your *memory* to recall, to be aware of experiences you have had of the Father; of the desire in your heart that the Father should be known and loved. Use your *intellect* to compare this desire with others that you have. Try to understand what this petition would mean to Jesus, how He would feel it. See if you have the same reasons He does to want the Father's name to be music in every human heart. Use your *will* to make Christ's desire, that the Father be known and loved, one with your desire. Rest in any good feelings or desires that come to you. Finally, see if any concrete actions suggest themselves and make any decisions that you think are good. Ask Our Lord to help you do what you decide on.

√ 3. Spend the last part of your prayer just repeating over and over to yourself slowly, "Our Father . . . who art in heaven . . . hallowed be thy name!" You might find it helpful to match the phrases with your breathing: saying "Our Father" as you breathe out, "who art in heaven" as you breathe in, "hallowed be thy name!" as you breathe out again. This "rhythmical prayer" is a good way just to savor and absorb affectively the truth and goodness you have already assimilated through memory, intellect, and will.

√ 4. Go through the same process for the other petitions of the *Our Father*. You can take one or several petitions in any one period of prayer. Also, if you like, you can close with rhythmical prayer using the whole *Our Father* instead of just one petition. Or sometimes you could use rhythmical prayer alone, without spending time meditating on the particular phrases. The guideline is to pray in the way that lets you best understand, appreciate, and savor the meaning of the Lord's Prayer and unite you heart most closely to its longings.

CHAPTER THIRTEEN

Achieving Unity Of Desire

How can we make the deep desires of our being what we really want them to be? How can we overcome the dividedness that makes us unable to desire with our whole hearts the goodness that we see and choose to desire? Is there a method — is there even the possibility — of building a whole heart?

There is a way. It is the way of *increasing faith* and *persevering prayer.*

When I was younger I would have suggested the way of "asceticism": of spiritual athleticism. I would have proposed schedules for nibbling away against spontaneous inclinations and appetites. For example, if you want to quit smoking, begin by smoking two less cigarettes a day, then four, etc. Or make a contract to run once around the block for every cigarette you smoke. Or smoke, but soak the tips of your cigarettes first in something that tastes foul.

This is the way of willpower. It is the strategy of frontal attack. The principle behind it is that if you are not strong enough to do something all at once, do it little by little. If you can't resist the temptation to do something you have decided not to do, then punish or penalize yourself every time you give in until your resistance grows stronger. This is the way of muscle.

Before I go any further, let me make clear that I am not rejecting this way. I believe that sooner or later, and to a greater or lesser extent, we do have to use this method. In the last analysis, and when push comes to shove, we just have to use our wills. We have to say yes or say no, and we have to just force ourselves to do it. Nothing makes difficult choices so easy that they just drop into our laps. And God did not create us to be wimps.

But now that I am older, with enough failures behind me to be somewhat wiser than I was before, I would not begin with willpower. I would begin with faith and prayer.

In the last three chapters we have spoken a lot about the motivation that comes from seeing, from understanding something. We proposed reflecting on the words of Jesus until they make more sense to us; weighing the reasons for what He proposes until they become so convincing that they motivate us; until they move us to actually go out and put His teaching into practice. The intellect is the guidance system of the will; where the intellect casts its light, the will is able to move.

GOING BEYOND INTELLECT

But sometimes intellect isn't enough. It might be because we are dealing with something whose reasons go beyond intellect; something coming from a motive, or directed toward a goal, beyond the range of human reason. An example of this would be the decision to truly live (and die) for something so vague, so unreal to our human perception, as "heaven," or the "kingdom of God." Or to base our whole lives, every choice and decision that we make, on desire to respond to "Jesus Christ." For this kind of choice we need to be guided by faith.

At other times we can understand perfectly well with our intellects the reasons for making a choice, but those reasons just don't have the power to move us. Although they are perfectly logical, they leave us absolutely cold. For example, I once read a book about the benefits of jogging that left me intellectually convinced I should jog. But I never have jogged. I suppose I am convinced that jogging is a good thing, but just not necessary for me — not here and now. If, however, a doctor examined my heart and told me I would be dead in a year if I did not start exercising more, then I think I would jog. And the more faith I had in the doctor's knowledge and sound judgment, the more motivated I would be to follow his advice. My faith in the doctor would convince me that jogging was not just a good thing in itself, but an essential thing for me personally, for me individually, in the concrete circumstances of my actual and unique situation in life. With my intellect I might see that the arguments for jogging are *true*; but what would make them *real* for me is the faith I put in the doctor.

It is like this in the spiritual life: it is my faith in Jesus Christ that makes His teaching real to me. The difference between accepting intellectually — and even with an assent based on God's word — that it would be good to dedicate my life to bringing about the kingdom of God on earth and actually desiring it, being totally motivated to do it, is the response I make in faith to Jesus Christ. If I really, deeply believe in Him as Teacher and Guide of my life, as the "Master of the Way," then when He says something is good I will be moved to do it. When He says, "Come," I will abandon "boat and father" — I will risk even my means of livelihood and my closest human and family ties — and follow. (See Matthew 4:8-22.)

"UNLESS YOU BECOME . . ."

We see this lived out every day in the faith children put in their parents.

Some children deeply believe — for some reason — that parents are to be trusted when it comes to teaching them how to live. So they really try, even when they are very young, to do what their parents tell them and advise them. They may take school seriously, for example, or stay away from drugs, or just try personally to be polite to people. And it pays off. They find that life is good to them. They have fewer problems; they are better adjusted; they do well in this world.

God promised it would be this way. To the commandment "Honor your father and your mother," God added a promise: "that you might have a long life upon earth." This is a Hebrew way of saying, "that your life might be full, happy, successful."

141

God promised that those who followed the guides He gave them would be better off for it.

Those children, on the other hand, who just never take seriously what their parents say — because they really don't place that much faith in them or in obedience — have to learn the hard way. They do all the things they were warned not to do, and they pay for it. They don't do what their parents are constantly urging them to do, and they lose out. Eventually they learn, but it costs them.

Children who really put faith in their parents, who really believe in obeying them, are able to act on their parents' advice out of true, interior conviction and desire. They follow their parents' counsels because they *want* to. And they want to because they believe it is for their good. As they put their parents' directions into practice, they experience for themselves the results. Then they don't have to believe anymore; they know. They have learned for themselves, but they learned the easy way.

If we really accept Jesus as Teacher, as Guide, as the "Master of the Way" to live on this earth, we too experience more and more for ourselves how right His teachings are. We come, not only to believe in them, but to "see" them. We can certify from our own experience that they lead to a greater fullness and happiness already in this life, over and above what we believe in faith about the next.

THE GIFT OF FAITH

To pursue unity of desire through the *way of increasing faith* is to focus first of all, not on the individual choices or goals we propose to embrace, but on relating in deep and positive faith to Jesus as Teacher, Leader, and Lord. And this is a choice in itself.

We may not be used to thinking of faith as a choice. That is because faith is first of all a gift. Faith is a sharing in God's own knowledge by sharing in God's own act of knowing. That is what faith is, and that is what "grace" means: the favor of sharing in the life of God. Because God lets us share in His life, we participate in God's own personal act of knowing, God's own personal act of loving. That is why faith is a pure gift: it is a sharing in the very life of God.

We can only share in God's life and action through His drawing us into Himself. This union with God in one shared life is called "grace," which means "favor," because it is a pure favor, a pure gift of God. There was no word in human language for this reality, because it was not part of creation; it was not a perceivable element of the natural world people found around them. So when God revealed the gift of grace through Jesus Christ there was no name for it. It was just referred to as "the favor," and that is how it is named to this day. Grace is the favor; it is *the* favor, the favor of all favors. And it is a pure, free gift. It has to be given by God; there is nothing we can do of ourselves to acquire it.

This favor of sharing in God's life manifests itself in us, and takes form in us, as *faith, hope*, and *love*. Graced faith is the gift and the act of sharing in God's own act of knowing. Graced love is the act of sharing in God's own act of loving. Graced hope is the act of fixing our desires on that fulfillment which belongs to God alone while trusting in Him to give it to us — and we can only do this by sharing in God's own act of intent. So faith, hope, and love are the active expression of grace, of the life of God, in our lives.

And these are free choices.

FAITH IS A CHOICE

It sounds like a contradiction in terms to say that faith is a pure gift and at the same time a free choice. It is both of these, however. God has to offer the gift; but we have to accept it. God gives us the power to decide in faith that Jesus Christ is a Teacher worthy of trust; but we have to make that decision for ourselves. We have to take responsibility for making that judgment in response to God's word.

The reason so many people remain so weak in faith, so inconsistent in living out their religion, so unmotivated by the words and example of Jesus, is just that they have never decided, deeply and personally for themselves, that they really believe in Jesus as the Teacher of Life. They have heard it. They do not deny it. But it doesn't mean very much to them personally. They may go to church — not to do that would be to take responsibility for another decision: the decision that Jesus is positively *not* the Guide they believe in — but their faith is more an act of conformity to other people's faith than a deep, personal judgment of their own.

The first step toward unification of our desires, therefore, is to decide deeply and personally that we really accept Jesus as Savior of the world and Teacher of Life. It is to choose Him concretely and practically as the "Master of the Way," the one whose teaching and example we will base our lives on.

To make this deep decision, however, is like kindling a fire: without immediate nourishment the fire will die out. When we start a fire, we have to start feeding twigs into it immediately: little ones first, then larger and larger ones, until the fire is able to absorb anything that is thrown into it.

Faith is like this: it has to be nourished by choices based on faith. We have to begin immediately to live out the teachings of Jesus in concrete, personal ways. If we believe in Him as Teacher, we have to look for something He teaches that we can put into practice right away — perhaps something small and easy that we know we can do, just as we search for twigs small enough to catch fire easily when we are kindling a fire. Once our response to Jesus is "Yes," we have to insist on forward motion.

NOURISHING FAITH

Try it. Jesus teaches that God is your Father: that God has made you His child, and that you can call God "Father" as truly as Jesus Himself can. Do you believe that? Then how do you act on this belief? Do you say the *Our Father* every day? Do you treat God, interact with God, as your Father? Do you try to keep the Commandments, for example, not because you "have" to, but because they are the guidelines your loving Father taught you to help you find happiness in life? Do you ever recite the Psalms — say, one a day — just because they are inspired hymns of praise and confidence in God and this God is your own Father?

Do you trust in the Father to provide for you? Do you express that trust by asking Him, specifically and concretely, for all the things that you need? Do you thank Him after you receive them? Do you thank Him for the day when you get up, and for all that the day has held for you when you go to bed?

If you believe God is your Father, then do you do what logically follows on this? Do you treat other people as your brothers and sisters? Do you do this, not heroically, but in specific, small acts of attentiveness that show your concern, that express your realization of bondedness with them? For example, is there anyone you just ignore? And when you hear someone criticized, do you respond to that — even when it is deserved — the way you would respond to criticism of your brother, your sister?

Do you believe that this whole world belongs to your Father? Do you ever pick up a piece of trash on the street, or in the place where you work, just because it is littering your Father's world?

Do you really believe that Jesus inspired the Gospels to provide you with guidance for your life? Do you choose to believe this, to make this specific judgment about them? Do you act on this judgment by reading the Gospels? For example, a little every day? Do you give any time to thinking about them? Five minutes? Ten? Is there any little thing you have begun to do as a result of something you read in the Gospels? Any change, however small, that you have made in your life which shows that you really have accepted Jesus as the Teacher of Life for yourself?

What about the sacraments? Do you believe Jesus Christ acts in them for you? Do you believe these are ways of encountering Jesus in human words and gestures? Ways of letting Him do for you — humanly and powerfully — what He desires to do? Then how often do you seek out these encounters with Him? In Communion? In Confession?

Do you believe that the Mass is a communal celebration of Jesus' act of love for us? Do you believe it is a priestly act on your part? That in the Mass all of us offer ourselves together with Jesus to the Father in reparation for sin and to give life to the world? If so, how actively do you participate in the celebration of the Eucharist? Do you sing? Do you join in the responses? Do you consciously offer yourself with the bread and wine to be placed on the altar and transformed? Do you unite yourself with Jesus on the cross when the host and the chalice are lifted up at the consecration/elevation, asking God to take you and use your life to bring His life to the world?

Do you believe Jesus is truly present in the host you receive in Communion? Then do you deliberately "commune" with Jesus at Communion time, speaking to Him, or just resting in deep, conscious awareness of His presence within you?

And then when you go out from Mass to work, or back to family life, are you conscious of being His embodied presence in the world? Do you try to do everything you do in partnership with Him, as His real Body on earth? What have you changed in your family life because you became more deeply aware that you were acting as His real presence, His real Body in your home? In your social life? Your professional or student life? In your civic and political involvement?

These are only a few examples of the way of increasing faith. They cost little (in most cases) and give much. They are simply ways of expressing in concrete actions the judgment we have made about Jesus Christ, the faith we have decided to place in Him. Every time we live out our faith, expressing it in real and concrete actions, we grow in faith; it becomes more real for us. This is the way of increasing faith, and it is the way to unification of our desires in response to the mystery of God.

ASKING ... AND ASKING

The *way of persevering prayer* needs little explanation. To keep praying is in itself an expression of faith, a concrete action in time and space that has no meaning except as an expression of belief in God or in the promises of Jesus Christ. If I keep asking God to make me pure in heart, undivided in my desire; if I keep thinking about the words of Jesus, trying to absorb them, to make His attitudes and values my own; if I do this perseveringly, day after day, without giving up, then my desires will change. I will find myself becoming more and more of one mind and one will with Jesus Christ. I will be transformed, not by my power but by His.

The Christian life is not just a discipline, a technique. It is a relationship, a continuing interaction with God. In this interaction it is above all God's action we rely on. We ask and He gives. We open ourselves (in response to His invitation) and He fills us. We present our desires (which He inspires in us) and He brings them to fulfillment. We have to cooperate, of course, and act with the strength God gives us. But all growth and movement come from God. That is why the beginning, middle, and end of all Christian progress come through asking, through prayer. Essentially, we become whole by asking God over and over again, every day, to make us whole.

Now the question is: Do I choose to make a decision about all this? To believe it and begin to act on it in some concrete way? Or do I choose to turn away from the question without answering at all? I entered into this retreat in order to change, and decisions are the only way to do that. So now it is time to make some.

A HELP TO RESPOND TO THIS CHAPTER:

1. Enter into prayer through the same "vestibule" we have used all along: awareness of the presence of God, physical ac-

knowledgment of what He means to you, prayer that He will help you see more clearly and respond.

2. Go through the questions in the last section of this chapter. Or use questions of your own that come to you. In response to these questions, write out your own "litany of faith and response." Say what you believe and how you are going to express that belief in action.

For example:

√ I believe in You, Jesus, as the Teacher of Life . . . Each day I will read and reflect on Your words.

√ I trust in You, God, as my Father . . . Each day I will present my needs to You and leave them in Your hands.

√ I believe, Lord, that I am Your presence, Your body on earth . . . Everything I do this day I will do in partnership with You.

(*Note:* The ways of expressing belief in action are necessarily rather vague and general in the examples above. In your own "litany of faith and response," try to decide on expressions of your faith that are real; i.e., that you can visualize yourself doing; that get down to the particulars of time and space.

(Think seriously and pray earnestly over this litany. It can be a significant moment in your personal history of response to God. Pray over it and write it out in your journal or elsewhere as the portrait of your soul.)

CHAPTER FOURTEEN

Union Of Heart:
The Way Of Passionate Response

IT IS CLEAR enough what it means to speak of union of mind and will with Jesus Christ. When we see and understand things the way He does, and desire what He does, embracing all of His ideals, values, and goals as our own, then we are one with Him in mind and will. But "union of heart" is a metaphor. Just what does "heart" refer to in this context? Which of our human activities or powers are in harmony with Christ's when we are "one in heart" with Him?

The word "harmony" might be the key. Union of heart presupposes union of mind and will. But it goes beyond these in adding a certain mutual resonance even on the emotional level. We are comfortable around those with whom we are one in heart. We can be ourselves with them. We sense what will make them laugh and cry, how they will feel in response to anything we do or say. And we sense this, not just because we know them well, but because we know from experience that they will react as we do and that we will react as they do.

We may not have begun this way. Our natural ways of reacting to various situations may have been very different when we first met. But through the experience of one another, by observing one another's reactions, understanding them and appreciating them, we have become able to share even one another's emotional responses to life. We have learned from one another to laugh at things we didn't laugh at before, to be sensitive to hurts to which we were insensitive before, to see beauty or ugliness where we didn't see it before, to be affected by things that did not affect us before, and not to be shattered now by things which formerly we could not handle. This is harmony of heart.

How do we arrive at or grow into this emotional harmony, this union of heart? I believe the key word is "spontaneity." When we have become so comfortable with each other, so trusting, so free, that we spontaneously express our thoughts, our feelings, our emotional reactions to things in each other's presence — and without any modifications or reserves — then we are able to grow together into union of heart.

OUR FEAR OF SPONTANEITY

Spontaneity is the key. Usually we edit what we express to others. If we don't think a particular emotion within us will be acceptable, or if we just don't think it will support the image of ourselves that we wish to project, we hide it. Or we disguise it. We manage to make it appear, in its external manifestation, a little different from what it is. For example, if I want to appear strong and self-sufficient, then I will not express my hurt to others by crying. I may put another twist on my hurt as it comes out and let it appear as anger instead. Or if I am nervous and insecure, I may disguise this feeling under a coat of bluster and arrogance. These are very common disguises, but all of us are adept at inventing new ones of our own. Sometimes our disguises are so subtle that we ourselves are unable to see through them.

Then we are "out of touch" with our emotions. We don't even have union of heart with ourselves.

With most people we do not express our emotions unreservedly. We tone them down a bit, or we dress them up in better clothes before we let them out of the house. We don't allow what is inside of us to just hang out. We don't let emotions pass into expression without exercising some control.

Control is the opposite of spontaneity. It is also the great neutralizer of passion. The more we insist on keeping a tight control over our self-expression, the less spontaneous we will be, and the more impossible it will be for us to abandon ourselves to passion.

CHOOSING REMOTE CONTROL

To be passionate is not to go against reason. But it is to take reason out of the driver's seat. We don't throw reason out of the car entirely; we just push it into the back seat, where it is able to intervene or we can call on it if things get out of hand. But while we are being passionate, our actions flow spontaneously; they come directly out of our gut or our feelings. Reason monitors them more or less remotely (or perhaps not at all, if we are so passionate that we are completely out of control), but we are not really thinking about what we are doing before we do it. We just act. We just express ourselves. We are spontaneous.

Union of heart depends on a deliberate decision to work at abandoning ourselves to spontaneity. It is not a contradiction in terms to speak of being "deliberately spontaneous." I can choose, reasonably and deliberately, to practice giving up control. A better expression might be to practice *suspending* control: I don't really give up control when I am spontaneous; I just relieve reason of direct command. I deliver myself over to spontaneity, like the commander of a ship stepping back and asking another officer to take the con. Then I allow myself to do and to say whatever comes to mind — or better, whatever I feel moved to do and say, without pausing to pass it through my mind, I let my feelings run the show.

To be a reasonable act, the deliberate choice to abandon myself to spontaneity must be based on an act of trust. And trust is an intellectual judgment. Before I can be rationally spontaneous, I have to know myself well enough to judge that I can trust myself not to do anything really foolish. I have to be sufficiently in touch with my feelings to have some idea where they will and will not lead me, and I have to know that I can rely on my reason to keep alert and to intervene if necessary to keep my feelings from just going wild. I also have to know my own deep desires and values well enough to judge that my will can be trusted

151

to accept the control of reason over feelings again should things begin to get out of hand.

I also have to trust the person with whom I am being spontaneous. When it comes to giving myself over to that spontaneity which leads to union of heart, trust in the other person is all important. I have to be confident I can trust the other not to mock me or make fun of me; not to look critically on what I might say or do; not to remain detached and aloof and under total control while I am abandoning myself to the experience of the moment. I have to trust the other to be just as abandoned and spontaneous as I am; to likewise let go of controls and to vibrate with me to the tune we are hearing together. But how does all this apply to seeking union of heart with Our Lord?

BEING PASSIONATE WITH GOD

Frequently — and more often than not, I would say — we are just as inhibited in our acts of self-expression to God as we are with other people. Ask yourself: when is the last time you cried in the presence of God? When is the last time you really laughed with Him? How spontaneously physical are you in your self-expression to Him? Do you ever pray alone in your room with your arms outstretched in the form of a cross? Or prostrate on your face on the floor? Do you ever dance for Him or with Him? Do you ever do crazy little things to show your love for Him?

It is hard to provide adequate examples here, because by definition when we are being spontaneous and passionate with Christ in private, our self-expression is private. It is very personal, and not something others are liable to understand or appreciate unless they have had the experience of being spontaneous and passionate with Him themselves. And then they don't need the examples! But I believe we have to include under this category of passionate response some of the extreme and even bizarre-sounding penances of the saints which have passed into public knowledge. St. Ignatius of Loyola, for example, got so carried away one time with sorrow for his sins (and apparently

152

he had some sins to be sorry for!) that he began beating himself on the breast with a rock. Two women who had befriended him picked him up later, near to death, and nursed him back to life. When Ignatius told the story, very reluctantly, years later in his autobiography, he obviously felt he had been carried away by his desire to express himself to God and had let his emotions take him past the stopping-point of prudence. He did not recommend the rock treatment to others!

All the saints and spiritual masters caution us not to go to extremes in penance. But many, if not most of them, went to extremes themselves. How do we explain this? Were they just imprudent people? Or were they inspired by God to go to these extremes because they were exceptions to the rule?

If the saints were really imprudent people, they should not have wound up saints, because imprudence in the spiritual life usually leads to discouragement and to other growth-inhibiting states of soul. The same is true of any compulsive behavior; people who practice exaggerated austerities in the spiritual life are suspected of acting out of some unconscious motivation which does not come from authentic love of God or lead to authentic love. No one becomes a free, loving, holy, and saintly person through rigid, compulsive, voluntaristic acts of self-punishment.

But if God inspired the penances of the saints, even by way of exception, then the saints were accusing God Himself of imprudence when later they said they should not have done what they did! How do we explain this?

A commonplace response is to say that the penances of the saints are to be "admired but not imitated." And this is a sound, practical principle. But why? Why should we admire something that was a mistake? And how do we explain the fact that so many saints did these exaggerated things, and that so many people who did these exaggerated things became saints? There would seem to be a connection.

LETTING THE DIVINE BECOME HUMAN

I believe the key to the explanation is in the words "spontaneity" and "passion." When St. Ignatius was thumping away with his rock, he was not coldly and deliberately punishing his body, like an officer in the old-time British navy impassively ordering up a killing number of lashes for a mutinous sailor. Nor was he inspired by God to beat himself half to death. He was simply giving human expression in a passionate way to what he felt within himself by grace. He was giving physical expression to a burning love, to a consuming desire to say to God how sorry he was that he had ever offended Him. Ignatius got carried away. His interior emotion was from God and the desire to express that emotion physically and passionately was a natural human reaction. But once Ignatius began to express what he felt, passion took over and its momentum carried him beyond what was reasonable. He almost killed himself.

What made Ignatius a saint was not the fact that he was carried away, but the fact that he was human enough, and let himself be human enough in his responses to God, to be subject to being carried away. He let himself be spontaneous and passionate with God. That is a natural, human thing to do. And it has its dangers. But the danger of not being spontaneous and of never being passionate with God is even worse. Not to be spontaneous is not to be a lover. And not to express ourselves physically to those whom we love is not to be fully human. The love the saints had for God was so intense that it could not be adequately expressed without some form of passionate, physical action. In their lives this often took the form of physical penance. They expressed themselves to Jesus using the same language He used to express Himself to us in His passion. But it was not the penances that made them saints. Nor was it just the love they had for God. It was the combination of loving God and *expressing* that love spontaneously and passionately that enabled them to grow in love to the level of heroic response to God. It was the love they *expressed* that made them saints.

THE INCARNATION FOREVER

Jesus, the model of all sanctity, the embodiment of total love on earth, was fully human and fully divine. What Jesus showed us was how divine love expresses itself in human terms, through human words and gestures, through everything alive and active in human nature. And in the saints we have Jesus expressing Himself again — as He does in every graced member of His Body on earth; that is, in all of us who believe in Him and have surrendered ourselves to Him in baptism. In the saints, however, the divine life of Jesus expresses itself most clearly, most strikingly, most unmistakably. That is the value and the role of the saints in the Church: to show us, to make evident to us, how the life of Jesus can express itself in various kinds of people, under different circumstances of time, place, and culture.

Without the saints — that is, without the clear manifestation of God's grace taking flesh in every time and place, within every human culture, in every variety and type of human person — we might wonder whether the Gospel is really relevant to our own times. We might be tempted to think that the grace of Christ and the ideals He preached can only work under special cultural conditions — like those of Jesus' own times, or in the Middle Ages, perhaps, but not in the world as we know it today. The saints give the lie to this. In the saints we find the divine expressing itself humanly again. And the human form of that divine expression is whatever fits and comes out of the culture, the times, the particular personality of each individual person in whom Jesus Christ is living and acting again. That is why there is such a variety of saints, and why the saints gave expression to their love for God in so many different ways, some of which seem bizarre and even objectionable to us in our particular culture.

TO GIVE FLESH TO CHRIST, GIVE EXPRESSION TO YOUR HEART

In the saints we find, not a series of models that we are called to imitate, but the general pattern that every one of us is called to follow: a pattern of the divine taking flesh in particular human ways. Each of us is called to be a clear and striking human embodiment of the presence and grace of Christ on earth.

Each of us is called to be a visible manifestation of the divine life of Jesus Christ expressing itself on earth today in the language and symbols of our particular culture, in the ways proper to each one of us as a particular, unique human person.

We can only do this, however, in the measure that we, like Him, are fully human and fully divine — and fully ourselves in giving expression to what is within us. We can only do it in the measure that we let the divine express itself humanly in us according to our own particular personalities and culture. The more spontaneously we allow that expression to take place, the more we surrender control to Jesus living within us and expressing Himself together with us according to all that we are, the more we will grow in union of heart with Him.

Spontaneity is the key to personal — even passionate — expression of ourselves to God. And personal, passionate expression of ourselves to God is the key to union of heart. Most of our self-expression to God is not passionate, however; nor do we usually begin with passion. We begin with the ordinary, daily things. We begin by letting our feelings find expression in little actions, little gestures of attentiveness to Him; gestures of faith, of trust, of love. A high-school girl in New Orleans resolved after her senior retreat that every morning when she awoke she would kneel with her arms outstretched in the form of a cross and recite the Morning Offering, dedicating all her thoughts, words, and actions of that day to Jesus Christ in love. The maintenance man at a convent in Memphis never passes by the chapel where the Blessed Sacrament is without genuflecting in the doorway. Another man I know in Memphis reaches out and touches the feet of the crucifix on the wall every time he enters and leaves his room. He has a lot of things to worry about, and this is his gesture of trust. I have known people who slept on the floor occasionally, because when they woke up during the night it helped them to think of Jesus. These are little things, but they are all personal things, and like the little gestures that become a private language between lovers, they keep our love for Jesus Christ alive. They keep our hearts sensitive to Him.

Then we in turn begin to pick up and to recognize the little ways in which He expresses love to us. This leads to union of heart with Him.

SUMMING UP:

✓ Harmony of heart comes through being spontaneous in the expression of ourselves with one another.

✓ We fear self-revelation. For this reason we hide behind disguises, "fronts," roles, images. And we are careful not to give up control.

✓ To deliberately choose to suspend control and to express our emotions spontaneously is a rational act. However, it presupposes trust in oneself and in those one is with.

✓ The passionate and sometimes imprudent gestures of the saints were simply acts of spontaneous human expression given to emotions aroused by grace. Because they gave human expression to the divine, and gave it passionately, they sometimes went to excess — and they became saints.

✓ We make Christ visible on earth today, and His good news credible, in the measure that we give spontaneous expression to the grace that is within us — and give it according to what each one of us is.

TO HELP YOU REFLECT ON THIS CHAPTER:

✓ Do you have any ways of expressing love for God in your daily life that are very personal to you? Are any of them so private in nature that you would feel embarrassed doing them in the presence of others?

✓ How often do you just give spontaneous expression to your faith or your love for God? Where, when do you do this?

Do you ever pray out loud in your own words? (For grace before meals, for example, or at the Prayer of the Faithful at Mass? At other times? With your spouse? Your children? A friend?) If not, why not begin?

√ Do you ever pray to God using body language: arms outstretched in the form of a cross, for example, or prostrate on the floor? Is kneeling down in church a form of body language? What is the difference between this and prostrating on your face?

√ Are you ever passionate in your expression of yourself to God? Do you feel moved or inspired by any of the passionate expressions of love which the saints gave to God? How many lives of saints have you read?

√ What would be the advantages of putting more spontaneity, or even passion, into your self-expression of God? Do you have any valid reason to fear this?

A PRAYER FORM TO PRACTICE: PRAYING WITH THE BODY

— 1. Enter through the usual "vestibule" of prayer. But when you make your physical acknowledgment of God's presence, kneel down and kiss the floor. (Obviously, this is a prayer to make in private.)

— 2. Keep kneeling with your forehead on the floor while while you ask God for help in making your prayer (third step of the "vestibule"). This will let your prayer begin already with the help of a more expressive body language (*Note:* Depending on the "tone" of your prayer — see below — you might want to use some other gesture. For example, if your prayer is going to focus on generosity and self-oblation, you could begin by extending your arms in the form of a cross and offering yourself to Our Lord. Tell Him you want to be His Body on earth, that you want Him to live in you, act in you, and use you according to His desire.)

— 3. Next, choose a "tone" for the prayer you want to make. That is, get in touch with your mood right now, and ask yourself what kind of interaction you want to have with God. Are you exhausted? Excited? Depressed? Grateful? Scared? Feeling passionate? Do you have the blahs? How would you describe the mood you are in right now?

— 4. Based on this, decide how you want to interact with God? Do you want Him to comfort you? Do you want to comfort Him? Praise Him? Adore Him? Offer yourself to Him? Do you want Him to inspire you and stimulate your mind? Do you just want to be comfortable in His presence for a while? To feel secure and safe? Romantic? Loved?

— 5. When you know how you want to interact with Him, continue your prayer in a physical position that expresses what you want to be most conscious of in God's presence during this time of prayer. This could be adoration, supplication, childlike trust, familiarity and comfortableness, self-oblation, or any other element or characteristic of your relationship with God.

— 6. If right now you don't have any other theme to pray over or scriptural passage to contemplate, try entering through your imagination into the scene from Luke 7:36-50, in which the repentant woman washes Jesus' feet with her tears and dries them with her hair. How do you feel as you watch this scene? Try to enter into it and interact with Jesus yourself according to whatever you feel.

Note: You can use these instructions in combination with any of the methods of prayer you have already learned during this retreat: meditation with memory, intellect, and will; contemplation through use of the imagination; "praying over prayers," rhythmical prayer, or any other. Praying with body language is not so much a method of prayer in itself as a way to lift up the affective tone of any method.

CHAPTER FIFTEEN

Communal Spontaneity

I ONCE WENT to watch a friend of mine named Jimmy Boudreaux ride a bull It was in a rodeo in Eunice, Louisiana, and the bull Jimmy drew was the meanest-looking bull I had ever seen. Apparently his looks were not deceptive, either, because every time someone mounted him and was thrown off (as everyone was) the rodeo hands could not drive the bull out of the arena; he would attack any horse and rider that came near him. The only way they could remove the bull was to let the whole herd back into the arena and drive them all out together. It taught me something about arriving at union of heart with God![1]

Sometimes we have so much resistance to spontaneity that we can't even begin. We don't know how. We are blocked. Something within us, like that bull in the arena, stares down or

---

[1]That's the end of the story. But in case you are wondering, Jimmy won the bull-riding event. It wasn't completely his doing, however. Because his bull was so mean, and because Jimmy's wife had just had a new baby (and because his other rodeo friends were worried about him), I had resolved to say a Hail Mary after every single performance in that rodeo until Jimmy rode. As it turned out, bull-riding was the last event in the rodeo, and Jimmy was the last rider in it. And it was a long rodeo! To this day Jimmy doesn't know that the real credit for his staying on that bull goes to me and the Blessed Mother!

chases away any emotion that tries to come to the surface and express itself. We are just hung up. Or numb.

The solution to this is to bring in the whole herd and take the obstacle away in the middle of it. We can learn spontaneity by letting ourselves be caught up in the spirit of a group. If we can find a group that celebrates, a community comfortable enough with one another to be free in their self-expression to God, then their spontaneity can give release to ours.

A NEW FOCUS ON COMMUNITY

This is a phenomenon of our times. Starting sometime in the sixties, the Church in the United States began to accept movements of personal, spontaneous faith-expression in groups. The first to which I was exposed was the Cursillo: a type of retreat in which the older tradition of silence and private meditation was replaced by discussion and free sharing by small groups seated at tables. In the Cursillo, people who had never before in their lives talked freely about their faith, or expressed any religious feelings in the presence of others, found that they were not alone. And they found, in the act of expressing themselves, that they had deep love for God, and deep desire to give themselves generously to Him. One after another I heard people say. "This is the first time in my life I have known what it is to be a Christian!" It isn't that they were not Christians already; it is just that they were not *aware* of it in all its length and breadth and height and depth, because they had never given conscious, free, spontaneous expression to what was latent within them.

Then came the charismatic renewal, the prayer groups. The key element in charismatic prayer in surrender to spontaneity. And it is the spontaneity in the group itself, the free expression of others, which teaches and enables each individual to be free.

Is this just a human, a psychological phenomenon? I do not think so. When people in grace — people who live by the life of God, people who have the Holy Spirit dwelling within them —

give spontaneous expression to their faith, their praise, their joy, it is not just they who are speaking. The light of faith is a sharing in God's own act of knowledge, and when we let that light shine out to others we are letting God speak His truth in us and through us. The love that is poured out in our hearts is the love proper to God Himself. When that graced love finds expression in us, whether in words, in gestures, or in deeds, it is God Himself who is declaring His love in and through our human actions. Then the presence of God becomes something discernible; something seen and heard and felt; something to celebrate.

PRECAUTIONS TO TAKE

Are there dangers in this? Yes, as we said in the previous chapter about passionate self-expression to God, there is always danger in spontaneity, always danger in giving up control. But there is even more danger in deadness. When people give spontaneous expression to their faith, their feelings, their religious impulses, there is always the likelihood that some of what they say, some of what they do, will not be from God. This is not likely to do any damage, however, so long as everyone is aware that this happens and no one takes anyone else's statement as an infallible pronouncement of the word of God, or anyone else's self-expression as an immediate and unmixed manifestation of the Holy Spirit. Discernment is necessary. As St. Paul said when he encouraged the early Christians to give free and spontaneous expression to their faith, we should rejoice that the prophets speak, but the rest of the group has to judge the reliability of what the prophets say. (See 1 Corinthians, chapter 14.)

And we might add, as a postscript, that the rest of the Church has the final judgment about what the group as a whole has to say!

Failure to do this has led in our day to many defections from the Church. Catholics have gone over in significant numbers to the fundamentalist, evangelical sects, the Bible churches, and self-styled "non-denominational" community churches.[2] They have done this, I believe, because they got so caught up in the exhilaration of an enthusiastic worshiping community that they were willing to suspend their powers of discernment and give up, not just doctrinal orthodoxy, but intellectual integrity for the sake of the emotional unity they experienced. The fundamentalists do not draw people through union of mind or will; that is, through deeper insight into the meaning of the Scriptures or through commitment to higher ideals. They draw people through an experience of union on the affective level; that is, by letting them feel warmth and oneness with others in the expression of faith and of love for Jesus. But since true union of heart is impossible without union of mind and will, those who want to keep experiencing this affective unity must sooner or later accept fundamentalist doctrine and commit themselves to the rules, the goals, and ideals of whatever group they are attached to. For these people, experienced union of heart is more important than truth or fidelity to the Gospel as such. And there you have a key to the Protestant Reformation.

A GUIDELINE TO FOLLOW: SPONTANEITY IS FOR THE STRONG

It may sound as if we are reversing our field here. We began by urging spontaneity, which implies a suspension of critical control. Now we are saying that by suspending their critical faculties and entering into the spontaneous religious expression of a fundamentalist group, many Catholics have been led right out of the Church. What, in practice, is the rule to follow here?

The answer to this dilemma is the same as the answer we

---

[2]A "non-denominational church" is a contradiction in terms. In reality, it just means a church that does not answer to any other group of believers for what it preaches or does. A non-denominational church is simply a new denomination that has not yet begun to spread out or accepted the responsibility of defining itself.

164

gave to the problem of passion. Passion also tends to sweep away intellectual judgment and take over the will. And so, when we surrender ourselves to passion, we must have reason to be confident that our intellectual judgment is strong enough to assert itself if things begin to get out of bounds, and that our basic commitment to the goodness and ideals we believe in is so deep that our wills will not abdicate to emotion. We also have to know the person or persons we are with, and be able to trust that they will not take advantage of our spontaneity to nudge us into a position we really do not want to be in.

In religious group expression, the same norms apply. If I know the group members are orthodox in their understanding of the Gospel and firm in their commitment to the Catholic Church, then I can deliver myself over to spontaneous faith-expression with them and not have to fear that the truth is going to be distorted. If I know the group is committed to the Church, I don't have to fear that my harmony of heart with members will separate me from the rest of the Body of Christ.[3]

When I do surrender myself to spontaneous religious expression with a group, I also need to be sure of my own faith — and specifically sure of my faith in the Church. The more firmly committed I am to Catholic doctrine, and the more deeply convinced I am in faith that the Catholic Church is the community established and preserved by Jesus Christ to be the authentic milieu of salvation until the end of time, the more I can afford to

---

[3]The term "Body of Christ" is broader than the term "Catholic Church," and includes all who have been incorporated into Christ through baptism, whether of water or of desire. But I take it as self-evident that the path toward union with the whole Body is through union with the original Church rather than through adhesion to separatist groups. The fundamentalists in general seem to be moving more toward separation and self-enclosedness than toward union and ecumenism. The opposite is true of the more established, serious churches who have a sense of accountability to fellow believers all over the world, regardless of denomination.

abandon myself to free faith-expression in a group. But if there is in me a latent anger at the Church, or if deep down I am not too sure there is any "one, true Church," then I may need to be careful. I may not be strong enough to pray safely and spontaneously with a group unless other members' faith is less flaky than mine.[4]

What we are saying in a nutshell is that just as we don't encourage adolescents to give themselves over to passion, because their judgments are not sufficiently sound and the commitment of their wills has not been tested enough to be relied upon, so we do not encourage people who know very little about their faith, or whose commitment to the Church is weak to begin with, to get involved in enthusiastic faith-expression with fundamen-

---

[4]If the last sentence angers you, you may be the kind of person I am worried about! For the past ten years I have been teaching in a Protestant seminary where at least nine different demoninations share love and respect for one another's beliefs, and I have firsthand knowledge of the truth and goodness that shine out in other Christian groups. But the Protestant communities, by and large, do not even claim to be communities established by Jesus Christ two thousand years ago to teach and minister authentically until the end of time the way the Catholic Church claims to be. Essentially, the Protestant denominations are groups of believers who band together in fellowship for mutual support in understanding and responding to the Gospel. This is a praiseworthy thing to do if, as a Protestant, you do not know the Church; or if, as a Catholic, you do not take a prayer group to be the Church itself. But if you are a Catholic, ask yourself about the logical consistency of saying there can be "more than one true Church." This is like suggesting that in Old Testament times there could have been more than one Chosen People. Or that the sum of two plus two might be both four and five. Either there is one true Church (one Church which Jesus Christ established and in which He promised to keep His teaching, His doctrine intact forever) or there is no true Church. If there is one true Church, the Catholics, with all of our faults and gropings, claim to be it! If we say there is no true Church, then all of us are Protestants already!

166

talist churches or flaky Catholic prayer groups. (Most of the Catholic prayer groups I know are not flaky at all, and the key to this seems to be good lay leadership and a strong linkage — usually through ordained priests — to hierarchical authority.) But in a normal group of orthodox, committed, and emotionally balanced believers, the more spontaneous and personal expression of faith there is the better. And without the help of a group like this, many people will never know what it is to experience and to feel union of heart religiously with others.

SPONTANEITY WITH OTHERS

Part of being spontaneous with Christ, therefore, is being spontaneous in expressing yourself to Him in the presence of other people. If we never allow ourselves to get excited about Jesus *with* other people, we may never experience what it is to be excited about Him at all. This is true of our human appreciation in general: until we celebrate something with others, or share with others a mutual response to it, we do not really feel how much it means to us. Suppose you had never celebrated Christmas any way except alone? Or your birthday? Or anyone else's birthday? How many times have you come to appreciate another person more because you celebrated that appreciation with a group of other people? Don't you even appreciate movies more when you watch them with a friend whose excitement communicates itself to you and with whom you can express your own excitement?

Is this what you experience when you express with others your appreciation for Jesus Christ? Does their excitement bring out your own? Does your excitement enkindle theirs? Have you ever experienced and felt what it is to appreciate Him communally with others? To celebrate together with others your experience of believing in Him, of trusting Him absolutely, of loving Him passionately?

When I was a pastor in Louisiana, a priest friend was once explaining the charismatic renewal to members of my parish. They asked him whether people did not get pretty emotional

167

during the prayer meetings. "Yes, they do," he said. "And they express it. But they get pretty excited during football games too and no one thinks it strange. Is it so strange that they would get excited about Jesus Christ?"

There you have it. It is pretty hard to believe that Jesus Christ is anyone to be excited about if the believers we know never get excited when talking about Him or celebrating what He means to them. It is hard to feel convinced that the Good News is all that good when nobody else seems to feel any enthusiasm about it. And how can we know what others feel unless they express it? How can others know what we feel if we do not express it?

Unexpressed faith is like a smoldering fire: it has no strength, no power, and it is hardly discernible even to the person who has it, until it is fanned into flame. Faith that is self-enclosed, like fire that is self-enclosed, just suffocates. It does not survive. This is a law of the spiritual life and a law of human life: all that is interior to us must find expression exteriorly or it dies out. People who never express love for other people become unloving. People who never show enthusiasm become apathetic. People who never express their emotions dry up — or their emotions find other ways, usually destructive, to force their way to the surface, and all sorts of psychological problems result.

So ask yourself about your freedom to be spontaneous in your expression of faith with other people. Is there anyone with whom you can pray out loud to Jesus in your own words? Is there any group with whom you can share openly and comfortably your thoughts about a Scripture passage you have read together? Have you ever tried? Have you ever thought about making a retreat that involves sharing? The Cursillo? Marriage Encounter? A Search or TEC retreat if you are younger?

Are you able during the Eucharistic celebration to break down and sing to God with other people? Or do you just stand there during the Mass, silent and detached from what is going on, refusing to contribute to the celebration? Are you free enough to express your own petitions during the Prayer of the

Faithful? Or do you leave it to the commentator to read the petitions some publisher of missalettes has printed up for the congregation that Sunday, letting the Prayer of the Faithful become by default the Prayer of the Whatso Publishing Company?

Union of heart with Jesus Christ is not identical with felt, experienced union of heart with other believers. But to express one's faith, one's hope, one's love for Jesus Christ spontaneously with others is one of the fastest, easiest ways to open oneself up to spontaneity with Him in private. And without some form of spontaneous, even at times passionate expression of response to Jesus Christ, we will never know completely what it is to love Him.

HOW TO PRAY OVER THIS CHAPTER:

√ Take the questions at the end of the chapter and think about them until you can answer them. If you are not expressing yourself at Mass, or not praying in a personal, spontaneous way with anyone else, ask whether or not you should begin. Don't let the first objections or difficulties that come to your mind decide the question for you. Give serious thought to it in the light of all that you have read in these last chapters about the value of spontaneity and communal expression of faith.

√ Begin your reflection with the ordinary "vestibule" of prayer, and end it talking to Our Lord in your own words.

CHAPTER SIXTEEN

NOW WHAT?

NOW THAT YOU are drawing to the end of this retreat, what do you do next?

I think this boils down to three questions:

√ What have you accomplished in the retreat so far?

√ What have you left unfinished in what you have considered so far?

√ Is there anything else you should reflect upon at this point?

I believe it is a necessary oversimplification to say that what you have accomplished in the retreat so far should be counted in *decisions*. What decisions have you made during the course of this retreat? Would you be able to write them down? Are they vague and general decisions, such as "I should pray more," or "I should be kinder to people"? Or are they so concrete and specific that you are able in your imagination to picture yourself doing what you have decided upon? Have you gotten down to the brass tacks of *when, where*, and *how* you are going to do what you have committed yourself to do? Until you do this your commitment is not real.

Would you be able to write down some decisions as down-to-earth as this, for example? "I am going to read Scripture for ten minutes every day, starting at 5:45 A.M., while drinking coffee in the kitchen." That decision is real; you can picture yourself doing it in time and space. Or: "I am going to resolve explicitly each morning as my feet hit the floor that this day I will try to do something life-giving for every person I meet, beginning with _____ and _____" (the names of the first persons you expect to meet that day). This decision is also real; you may not know exactly how you are going to be life-giving to each of these people, but you know when, where, and with whom you are going to look for a way, and to look is already a concrete act. Besides, you know some concrete things you can do if nothing else suggests itself at the time: you can smile, for example, or just say something complimentary. You can picture yourself carrying out this resolution in a number of concrete ways. It is real enough to be pictured in the imagination. That means it is real enough to be lived out.

How many decisions like this have you made during the course of this retreat? Have you written them down anywhere? Would you be able now to pick them out of your journal and make a list of them?

If you make such a list, it will be easy for you to go over it from time to time (no, that is too general: *when*, concretely — that is, at what time of day, and on what days of the week or month will you go over it?) in order to check on your performance and keep these decisions alive and active in your life.

Also, to make the list now will give you a sense of having accomplished something real during this retreat. It will show you that you have not been wasting your time. Even if you have not lived out your decisions very well yet, just to have made them gives you a concrete plan of action for your spiritual life.

That is the first step: to ask what you have accomplished during this retreat and to be specific about it. If you have done this, if you have been able to identify some concrete, time-and-space actions you are resolved upon, it would be good now to ask about another category of decision: the decisions you have made that are simply deep, definitive, explicit acts of personal judgment and of faith.

WHAT HAVE YOU CHOSEN TO BELIEVE?

Have you decided, for example, that you have an ultimate, rock-bottom foundation of value as a human being which you cannot lose so long as you have one more word of choice left to speak on this earth, and that this value is simply your *capacity* to respond freely and greatly to life? Have you accepted, as an act of personal judgment and decision, that God truly loves you? That He chooses and desires to invest everything He is in what you are able to become? Do you accept His love? Do you agree that you are worth everything He invests?

Do you understand fulfillment in life to consist in creating yourself as a person by choices? Do you believe that every free choice you make determines the shape of your soul? And do you believe that when you reverse a choice by repentance it is no longer a part of you? That the sins of the past no longer enter into the "who" that you are as a person? That they no longer affect the meaning of your name?

Have you really decided to make these truths the foundation on which you stand? Have you thought about them concretely enough to see how they should affect your everyday attitudes and choices? Do you know how you can live them out? Have you adopted them as your working philosophy of life and included them in your response of faith to the message of Jesus Christ?

Have you really accepted to look upon everything in life — everything you do and everything that happens to you — as nothing but an *occasion for response*? And have you decided, deeply and strongly, that your life on this earth cannot be saved — from destructiveness, distortion, meaninglessness, or mediocrity — unless you make interaction with Jesus Christ a part of it in everything you do? Part of your personal life, family life, social life, professional or student life, your civic and political involvement?

These are not all the deep, intellectual judgments and faith-decisions that have been proposed throughout this retreat. But these are enough to make clear what we mean when we speak of a category of decision which is not a choice to do some concrete, particular thing in time and space, but simply a choice to believe. This decision is concrete, however, in that it is a choice to believe something quite specific, which has very practical overtones. It implies the choice to base your concrete action choices on what you have chosen to believe. It also includes the resolution not to entertain doubts any more, and not to sit by passively when your mind is overrun by thoughts and feelings that are contrary to what you have chosen to believe. When you have really chosen to believe something — when you have made up your mind — you fight off contrary thoughts and feelings as invaders. You may not be able to throw them out entirely all the time, but you can refuse to simply abdicate and let them take over the territory of your consciousness. You can resist by sending your own opposing thoughts to the front.

It would be good to make a list of these decisions too: of the ideas you have deeply accepted, and the principles you have decided to live by, to base your choices on. This list can serve as a kind of personal *credo* or profession of practical faith. To write down and get into focus the truths you are willing to live by is a good way to come to a deeper, clearer understanding of who you are as a person — and of how this retreat has influenced that.

IS ANYTHING HANGING OVER?

This leads us to our second question: Is there anything you have left incomplete in this series of reflections, in this process of confirming or reforming the basic structure of your attitudes and values? Is there anything you need to think about some more? Are there decisions you have faced but not yet made? Are there some decisions you have tabled, that you have not even wanted to confront yet? In other words, are there some thoughts or chapters in this book that you need to go back over, on which you need to spend more time?

If so, do it. Spend all the time on this retreat that you need to spend in order to make it work. One advantage of making a retreat in private like this, using a book, is that you can go at your own pace and spend as long on any one thought as you desire. No one is rushing you. It is better to come to terms with a few deep, foundational principles and guidelines, and to make them a working part of your life, than to read and react momentarily to a whole lot of exciting ideas that just make you feel good. Thoughts don't change our lives; choices do. Until knowledge passes into action, it is like gasoline in your tank: it gives you a lot of possibilities, but it doesn't get you anywhere. So go back over any unfinished reflection this book has aroused until you are able to make it a working part of your life; until it becomes a foundation for your choices.

Did you underline or highlight passages in this book which struck you as you read? If so, you might glance over these lines again to see how many of them contain thoughts you want to look at longer, until you can integrate them into your life, make them a part of your personality.

If you have not underlined or even if you have, you may want to just read through this book again, seeing whether all the ideas in it are familiar to you now; whether you feel that you own them, have appropriated them, are comfortable with them. This second reading can be a kind of "contemplation run": a time just to look at what you have already labored to understand and to integrate into your life, and now are able just to contemplate with affirmation and peace.

This brings us to our third question: Is there anything else, anything new, any further idea that you should turn to and begin to reflect upon at this point? In other words, where do you go from here?

WHAT ARE YOUR NEEDS?

There are three ways to come to an answer to that question. The first is to ask what your personal needs are at this point. Do you yourself feel the need to go on to any particular consideration, or to move into any particular area or response to the message of Jesus? In the spiritual life, appetite is an important element of the guidance system: the first place to look is toward the fulfillment of your felt desires.

I cannot help you very much through this book to identify those desires or to find the first step toward fulfilling them. That might be something that requires personal direction and coaching. For this you can consult some spiritual friend, your pastor, your confessor, or anyone who has experience in living the spiritual life consciously and consistently, especially if it is someone who knows you. A good source for this kind of help would be a holy nun: one who seems to be happy in her religious life, not just because she is involved in work she likes, but because she has that special radiance of a person who is loved and who loves. Sometimes a Sister who is retired or semi-retired, if she shows the "fruit of the Spirit" that should characterize Christian old age, is a good person to contact, because the retired have both experience and time to share.[1]

WHAT IS THE NEXT LOGICAL STEP TO TAKE?

The second way to find the next step is to take the systematic approach: What is the next *logical* step to take after this one? In the process of giving oneself totally to Jesus Christ, what logically follows the decision to base one's whole life on personal relationship with Him? Once I have decided to make interaction with Jesus Christ the starting point and foundation of everything I do, decide, and desire in my personal life, family life, social life, business (or student) life, and civic life, where would I normally go from here?

The answer to this is to find and adopt a particular *spirituality*.

A "spirituality" is simply a path, a way to get somewhere. All Christian spiritualities lead to the same goal: the perfection of graced faith, hope, and love in total union of mind and heart and will with Jesus Christ. But there are different ways to arrive at the goal, although the Way that every way must follow, and the essential ingredient of every Christian way, is the hu-

---

[1]The fruit of the Spirit includes love, joy, peace, patient endurance, kindness, generosity, faith, gentleness, and self-control. See Galatians 5:22-23.

manity of Jesus Himself, who is the Way, the Truth, and the Life. We come to the Father through interaction with the humanity of Jesus, and through this same interaction with Jesus we receive from Him and from the Father the gift of the Holy Spirit.

It is through Jesus that we come to the fullness of graced life. But Jesus can lead one person to the top of the mountain by one path and another person by another path. It is a matter of where you put your feet first and which approach will be easier for you.

Some spiritualities concentrate on prayer, or on using a particular method of prayer. Some put their emphasis on overcoming faults and developing virtues. Some begin with healing. Some concentrate on releasing, activating, and experiencing the gifts of the Holy Spirit. Some spiritualities work mostly through solitude and private encounter with God; others through community and communal expression of response, through celebration and liturgy. And all spiritualities, to be whole, will in some way incorporate all of these elements in some degree or another, under one form or another.

The spirituality I follow and propose to others works through *decisions*: through a series of graded commitments. It is a spirituality of growth by objectives: it keeps us moving by encouraging us to aim at one objective after another. And each objective is a choice: an explicit, personal commitment made with clear understanding and deep determination.

Basically there are five of these decisions. All are implicit in our baptismal commitment; all are essential to leading a whole, an authentic Christian life. They are:

√ 1. The commitment to base one's whole life on personal relationship (interaction) with Jesus Christ. This is what it means to be a *Christian*.

√ 2. The commitment to lead a life characterized by reflection on the message of Jesus Christ. This is what it means to be a *Disciple*.

√ 3. The commitment to lead a life of prophetic witness to

177

Jesus Christ. This is really a commitment to a life of continual conversion (change): to a lifelong effort to keep embodying the Gospel more and more authentically in one's lifestyle and in all of one's choices. This is what it means to live out one's baptismal consecration as *Prophet*.

√ 4. The commitment to mediate the life of God to others by giving human expression to the divine faith, hope, and love that is within us. This is an acceptance of Christian community, and it is what it means to live out one's baptismal consecration as *Priest*.

√ 5. The commitment to take responsibility, as faithful stewards of the kingship of Jesus Christ, for establishing His reign over every area and activity of human life. This is a commitment to the apostolate of transforming the world, and it is what it means to live out one's baptismal consecration as *King*.

The way of growth I propose is simply a process of focusing on these commitments, one after another, until I come to embrace and to live out each one in all of its breadth and length and height and depth.

HOW CAN I SHARE THIS WITH OTHERS?

Finally, the last suggestion I would make for finding out how to proceed from this point is for you to ask, "What can I do to share with others what I have seen and learned? What can I do to help others become more deeply involved with Jesus Christ as this retreat has helped me to do?"

It is just a fact of the Gospel that the first reaction of those who really encountered Jesus Christ was to share that experience with others. When Andrew first met Jesus, he went looking for his brother Simon to bring him into the same relationship with Jesus he had found. When Jesus called Philip, the first thing Philip did was go to his friend Nathanael and insist that he come to meet Jesus too. The woman Jesus met at the well in Samaria did the same thing: she brought the whole town to Him (see John 1:15-52; 4:4-42).

Besides being the natural, spontaneous reaction of those who truly encounter Jesus, the act of bringing others into relationship with Him is one of the most reliable ways of remaining in an active relationship with Him oneself. Most people who grow in knowledge and love of Jesus Christ do so in company with others. When it comes to persevering in the spiritual life, mutual support or mutual encouragement is the name of the game. Jesus is invisible to us, but visible friends can make His presence real and experiential through the visible response we see them making to Him in their actions.

So you might think of how you can join together with one or two other people in order to be disciples together and to encourage one another along the road to deeper intimacy with Him. What is the first step you can take toward doing this?

And now it is your turn again. What is your next step? What step do you choose to take?[2]

HOW TO RESPOND TO THIS CHAPTER — AND TO THIS RETREAT

To bring this retreat to the kind of conclusion which will make it a new beginning of spiritual growth in your life rather than just an episode, go through this last chapter again slowly. Take time to answer the questions it asks. These questions fall into three categories:

√ 1. Ask what you have accomplished in this retreat so far. Make the list of concrete decisions and of specific beliefs or convictions described in the first pages of this chapter.

√ 2. Ask what ideas you have seen in the retreat or inclina-

---

[2]If you want to follow the plan of spirituality I have outlined above — the commitment to be *Christian, Disciple, Prophet, Priest,* and *King* — or if any one of these commitments interests you, I can supply both books for personal reading and meeting plans for communal discussion and prayer. For further information, write me at His Way Communications, c/o the Monastery of St. Clare, 1310 Dellwood Ave., Memphis TN 38127.

nations you have felt that you need to follow up on. Check what you have highlighted as you read, the notes you have made in your journal, and ask if there is any thought or inclination within you that is making you feel uneasy. You may want to reread this book to see if you are comfortable now with everything in it.

√ 3. When you are satisfied that you have adequately absorbed and responded to the ideas in this book, ask what you want your next step to be.

- What are your personal needs at this point?

- What is the next logical step to take from here? Have you found any spirituality or path to growth in the spiritual life that you feel drawn to follow? How would you set about following that path?

- Is there any way you can share what you have learned with others or help yourself to keep growing by helping others to grow? Should you try to interest some others in reading or praying or discussing the spiritual life with you?